RECORDS OF THE IRISH CATHOLIC CHURCH

Maynooth Research Guides for Irish Local History

GENERAL EDITOR   Mary Ann Lyons, St Patrick's College, Drumcondra

This pamphlet is one of three in the newly instituted Maynooth Guides for Local History series. Written by specialists in the relevant fields, these volumes are designed to provide historians, and specifically those interested in local history, with practical advice regarding the consultation of specific collections of historical material, thereby enabling them to conduct independent research in a competent and thorough manner. In each volume, a brief history of the relevant institutions is provided and the principal primary sources are identified and critically evaluated, with specific reference to their usefulness to the local historian. Readers receive step by step guidance as to how to conduct their research and are alerted to some of the problems which they might encounter in working with particular collections. Possible avenues for research are suggested and relevant secondary works are also recommended.

I wish to acknowledge the support and interest in this series shown by Dr John Logan, University of Limerick and the valuable input of Dr Raymond Gillespie, N.U.I. Maynooth and Dr Jimmy Kelly, St Patrick's College, Drumcondra.

Maynooth Research Guides for Irish Local History: Number 3

Records of the Irish Catholic Church

Patrick J. Corish
&
David C. Sheehy

IRISH ACADEMIC PRESS
DUBLIN • PORTLAND, OR

First published in 2001 by
IRISH ACADEMIC PRESS
44, Northumberland Road, Dublin 4, Ireland
and in the United States of America by
IRISH ACADEMIC PRESS
c/o ISBS, 5824 NE Hassalo Street, Portland, OR 97213–3644.

website: www.iap.ie

© Patrick J. Corish & David C. Sheehy 2001

British Library Cataloguing in Publication Data
Corish, Patrick J. (Patrick Joseph), 1921–
 Roman Catholic records. – (Maynooth guides for local history research)
 1. Catholic Church 2. Church records and registers – Ireland
 I. Title II. Sheehy, David C.
 929.3'415
 ISBN 0–7165–2698–0

Library of Congress Cataloging-in-Publication Data
Corish, Patrick J., 1921–
 Roman Catholic records/Patrick J. Corish & David C. Sheehy.
  p. cm. — (Maynooth guides for local history research)
 Includes bibliographical references and index.
 ISBN 0–7165–2701–4 (paperback)
  1. Ireland—History, Local—Sources—Handbooks, manuals, etc. 2. Northern Ireland—History, Local—Sources—Handbooks, manuals, etc. 3. Catholic Church—Ireland—History—Sources—Handbooks, manuals, etc.
 I. Sheehy, David C. II. Title. III. Series.
 DA905 .C67 2000
 941.5—dc21   00–025014

All rights reserved. Without limiting the rights under copyright reserved alone, no part of this publication may be reproduced, stored in or introduced into a retrieval system, or transmitted, in any form or by any means (electronic, mechanical, photocopying, recording or otherwise), without the prior written permission of both the copyright owner and the above publisher of this book.

Typeset in 10 pt on 12 pt Bembo by
Carrigboy Typesetting Services, County Cork
Printed by ColourBook Ltd., Dublin

Contents

List of illustrations vi

Introduction 1

1 Records in archives outside Ireland
  Patrick J. Corish 3

2 Records in archives in Ireland
  David C. Sheehy 27

Conclusion 45

Appendices 47

List of Illustrations

1. Archbishop Paul Cullen to Tobias Kirby, rector of the Irish College, Rome, 4 November 1855 (Irish College, Rome: Kirby papers, Add MSS 1/2/106) — 15

2. Map 1 Irish colleges abroad — 19

3. Oath taken by John Wadding of Wexford, 18 October 1601, at his admission to the Irish College, Salamanca, giving details of his previous life and education (Maynooth College Archives, Salamanca Papers 1/1/5) — 21

4. Map 2 Catholic dioceses of Ireland — 26

5. Visitation return for the parish of Blanchardstown, 1830 (Dublin Diocesan Archives) — 30

6. Extract from the Confraternity Minute Book, parish of SS. Michael and John, Dublin, 1873 (Dublin Diocesan Archives) — 34

7. Essential works for researchers to consult: *Irish Catholic Directory, Archivium Hibernicum,* and *Collectanea Hibernica* — 44

Introduction

Since the destruction of the Public Record Office of Ireland in 1922 historians have been obliged to turn to institutions outside the State sector in Ireland, for alternative archival sources. The Catholic Church, being the largest Christian denomination in this country and possessing a substantial administrative structure, is, consequently, a significant creator of records. The archives of the Church represent, for the local historian, both a challenge and an opportunity. The challenge is posed, firstly, by problems relating to access, which arise from a legacy of neglect and the continued under-resourcing of archival services; by difficulties in obtaining accurate published information on those records which *are* available to researchers; and by the fact that for the period from the Henrician Reformation in the mid-1530s down to the second half of the eighteenth century the researcher must look *outside* Ireland for Catholic sources relevant to events which took place in Ireland. An additional obstacle is represented by the fact that during the period between the Council of Trent (1545–63) and the Second Vatican Council (1962–68) much of the business of the Church was conducted through Latin, Italian and French. The opportunity arises from the fact that though researchers are familiar with one particular portion of the Church's corpus of archives, namely parish registers, a whole range of other records, some of which are of direct local historical interest, have, up until now, hardly been utilised.

I. ADMINISTRATIVE STRUCTURE

The institutional structure of the Catholic Church in Ireland consists of a diocesan system of organisation with a parallel network of religious congregations and societies formed into provinces. The diocesan system has been in place since the twelfth century. A total of twenty-six dioceses, of varying size and population, are grouped under four provinces: Armagh, Cashel, Dublin and Tuam. The provinces are headed by four metropolitans, or archbishops, with the remaining twenty-two suffragan or subordinate dioceses arranged under their respective jurisdictions. Armagh, as the primatial see, is the most important diocese, in terms of ecclesiastical prestige; Tuam has the largest extent of territory, while Dublin is both the most populous and encompasses the centre of secular political gravity. Each diocese oversees a further layer of pastoral administration – based on the parish. In 1999, the twenty-six dioceses in Ireland embraced close on two thousand parishes. In addition, some dioceses possess diocesan seminaries or colleges. These are generally establishments of long standing which not only house important records created by each institution but also serve as places of deposit for invaluable local historical collections.

II. THE CHURCH'S ARCHIVES

The keeping of archives at diocesan and parochial level is today an essential requirement of administration, as stipulated by the Code of Canon Law – the body of legislation governing the administrative procedure of the Catholic Church throughout the world, and by regulations laid down at national and provincial synods in Ireland. However, the survival of records, down through the centuries, has been complicated by the Church's own turbulent history, especially since the Reformation, and by the tardy development of archival consciousness among Church personnel responsible for the creation and custody of archives.

Only a very small portion of the Church's archives, for the period from the mid-sixteenth to the mid-eighteenth centuries, still survives in Ireland today. However, as Patrick J. Corish explains, documentation of relevance to Irish local history for this very period does survive in Catholic archival repositories outside Ireland. In contrast, since the second half of the eighteenth century, a considerable body of records has accumulated, within all levels of the Church's administrative structure in this country, presenting a rich and varied source for the study of Irish local history. The purpose of this guide is to provide researchers with an introduction to these two distinct bodies of archives. In the first section, Patrick J. Corish surveys the rich holdings of relevant Church and State archival repositories in the United Kingdom and on the Continent. He identifies the main series of records of Irish research interest, delineates the historical background to their creation or acquisition, and guides the reader in the direction of related published guides, reports, and calendars. In the second section, David Sheehy examines the archives of the Church which have accumulated in Ireland since the eighteenth century, under four headings: diocesan archives, college archives, parish archives and religious archives. In the case of each category, there is a discussion of the historical background to the creation and preservation of the particular archives; the nature and extent of archival holdings is elucidated, and the problems and possibilities associated with researching the material are also discussed.

The authors hope that this short volume will alert researchers to the importance of Catholic sources in Ireland and overseas for the study of Irish local history. We also hope that it will assist them in gaining a clearer understanding of the range and nature of the Church's archives and a realistic appreciation of the possibilities of being able to access and exploit this material.

Records in archives outside Ireland

It is hard to be certain to what extent ecclesiastical records were regularly kept in Ireland before the Reformation. The very fact that, in the words of a contemporary, it was 'a land of so much long continued war within itself' would suggest that what records were kept were in serious danger of destruction. The sixteenth and seventeenth centuries were marked by radical disruption of the traditional patterns of society. The domestic church records that survived all this ended in the custody of the Church by law established, the Church of Ireland. Further, during the seventeenth and eighteenth centuries the Catholic Church in Ireland was justifiably anxious about keeping records. This resulted in the anomalous situation that for these two centuries in particular the great bulk of the Catholic records were created and preserved by an extensive exile community in Catholic Europe. This community was widely scattered, and so are the records. Rome in naturally the principal focus, and here, of course, the records go back before the Reformation. Another major focus was London, the seat of the royal administration. The London Public Record Office is a rich source of information, and here too the records go back to medieval times.

I. LONDON AND THE PUBLIC RECORD OFFICE

It will be convenient to deal with the London records first. These would always have been important, because Ireland was either a dependent kingdom or a kingdom united with Great Britain, though it retained a separate administration even when united. What made these London records of even greater importance was, of course, the destruction of the Irish Public Record Office in 1922. How much 'grassroots' detail for the history of the Catholic Church in Ireland was lost with it, particularly for the eighteenth century, will appear, for example, from W.P. Burke, *Irish Priests in the Penal Times 1660–1760* (Waterford 1914, reprinted Shannon, 1969). This book in substance consists of extracts from the correspondence between the local authorities and the central administration in Dublin. All this is now lost, so the historian has to depend on the correspondence between Dublin and London. It will be clear that the loss is particularly serious for the local historian.

Ecclesiastical material is scattered through the general records of the London administration. These records will be dealt with in detail in another context, and here it must suffice to call attention to the great series of calendars published by the Stationery Office in London, as detailed in *British National Archives: Sectional List 24*. Interest in Church affairs in Ireland reflects the aims and interests of government at the time. From the Norman invasion in the twelfth century to the Reformation in the sixteenth these interests will, by and large, be concentrated on provisions to major ecclesiastical benefices in those parts of the country controlled by the Dublin government, *ecclesia inter Anglicos*. The change in the sixteenth century was profound. There was not merely a Tudor revolution in religion: there was also a Tudor revolution in government. This was reflected especially in the rise of the secretariate. From this change flows the great series of Calendars of State Papers, with an exclusively Irish series from 1509 to 1670 (S.P. 63, 32 volumes of calendars). It should be noted that a project is now under way to provide a replacement for the totally inadequate first volume, covering the years from 1509 to 1573. After 1673 the Irish papers, and their calendars, are merged in the general series 'State Papers Domestic'. With the increasing complexities of secretariate and government the system threatened to get out of control. It was saved by a complete overhaul in 1782. In the present context it must suffice to call attention to a small but very useful book: *Irish History from 1700: a Guide to Sources in the Public Record Office* by Alice Prochaska (London, 1986).

In the years of imperial resources and cheap printing the British government envisaged the calendaring of all records relating to the United Kingdom wherever they might be found, whether in the jurisdiction or outside it. From within the United Kingdom there appeared two series of calendars with particular relevance for the history of the Catholic Church in Ireland. One was the *Calendar of Carew Papers in the Lambeth Library* (6 vols, London, 1867–73). These cover the years from 1515 to 1624, paralleling and in many instances duplicating the material in the State Papers. They can be particularly useful for the years before 1573, when the calendar of the latter is so inadequate. The collection known as the Stuart Papers is of even greater interest. These papers originated with the exiled Stuart monarchy, and for the most part chronicle their increasingly hopeless attempts to recover the throne. These attempts may be regarded as finally extinguished in 1766, with the death of the man known to his supporters as James III and to his opponents as the Young Pretender. When he died the papacy had been about his only supporter, and papal support was not extended to his elder son, Prince Charles Edward. When he in turn died in 1788 the papers passed to his younger brother, Henry cardinal of York and bishop of Frascati. Henry was reduced to great poverty after the French occupation of Rome in 1796. He accented a pension from King George III in 1800, and that same year he returned to Frascati, where he died in 1807 at the age of eighty-two. King George IV (1820–1830) purchased the papers for the crown, and they have since been at Windsor Castle. They are on microfilm in the British Library and the University of London library. The collection is now covered by good calendars for the years in which the Stuarts had political importance: *Stuart MSS at Windsor Castle* (Historical Manuscripts Commission, 7 vols, London, 1902–23), covering the years from 1579 to 1718; and Patrick Fagan (ed.), *Ireland in the Stuart Papers* (2 vols, Dublin, 1995), covering the years from 1719 to 1765.

The Stuart Papers have considerable potential for the local historian for a period when other sources for the history of the Catholic Church in Ireland are thin on the ground. It is unflattering but true that they show that Ireland was marginal to the wider political interests of the Stuarts in exile, that they even made little enough of that prerogative of royalty that they clung to until it was taken from them by the papacy, the right to present candidates for the Irish Catholic episcopate. But if Irish interests were remote from the Stuarts, the Stuarts were very central to the Irish, at least to the Irish exiles in Catholic Europe. In consequence, the Stuart Papers have extensive and detailed reports on the state of affairs in Ireland, and also on the Irish colleges on the continent, which, as will be seen, developed into what might be called social centres for the Irish abroad in addition to their primary function as ecclesiastical seminaries. Overall, there are real pickings for the local historian of Irish ecclesiastical affairs, in a source which has not been exactly overused.

It will be noted that the calendars of the Stuart Papers to 1718 were published by the Stationery Office for the Royal Commission on Historical Manuscripts. This had been set up in April 1869 to report on and prepare calendars of manuscripts in private hands or in the hands of various corporations. The Commission was closely linked with the Public Record Office, the Master of the Rolls being chairman and the Deputy Keeper of the Records a member. The only Irish member of the original commission was Charles W. Russell, formerly professor of ecclesiastical history at Maynooth and at this time president of the college. It was through his influence that Maynooth College Library secured ('with the compliments of the Master of the Rolls') its magnificent sets of the Calendars of State Papers and of the publications of the Historical Manuscripts Commission. These latter are especially to be treasured, for they are almost without exception out of print (*HMSO Sectional List 17: Publications of the Royal Commission on Historical Manuscripts*). Individual volumes are well indexed, and there is a general index of places and persons, but there is no short cut or quick guide to what the local historian may hope to find in this vast collection. It includes reports and calendars concerning Irish families and institutions (the most extensive dealing with the papers of the marquis of Ormond), as well as those of their counterparts in England who in one way or another were involved in Irish affairs. And here it is impossible to go into detail about the more recent developments. As more and more papers left their stately homes for public custody, and papers of lesser figures came in increasing quantity, the printed report or calendar tended to be supplanted by a vast card index at headquarters in London, which in turn was computerised.

II. THE PUBLIC RECORD OFFICE AND THE VATICAN ARCHIVES

In the days of cheap printing and imperial finances the British Public Record Office extended its search for sources to records outside the jurisdiction, and printed extensive catalogues of documents in foreign archives. The series of seventeen volumes extracted mainly from the Spanish state archives at Simancas and covering the years of the Tudor monarchy (1485–1603) is worth bearing in mind. But by far the most important of these ventures from the point of view of the local historian of the Irish Catholic Church is the work done in the Vatican Archives by the British Public Record Office (and continued in more recent years by the Irish Manuscripts Commission). This has resulted in the *Calendar of Entries in the Papal Registers relating to Great Britain and Ireland (Papal Letters* (19 vols, London, 1894–1998); *Petitions*, 1 vol. (1897)).

The Public Record Office in London and the Vatican Archives seem an unlikely combination, but the project grew naturally out of developments in the nineteenth century. The French Revolution had given currency to the idea that the 'secret' archives of governments should be open to historical investigation, and the Emperor Napoleon had gathered archives from all over Europe into Paris in a grandiose vision of a huge central imperial archive. The archives of the Vatican were among those brought to Paris. Like all the others they were returned after the downfall of Napoleon, and like all the others some volumes were returned to the wrong place or just went missing. In the recent excitement about the opening of the archives of the Inquisition nobody seems to have adverted to the fact that quite a number of volumes from this collection, and also some volumes of papal letters, are among the manuscripts in Trinity College. They were bought in Paris by an English aristocrat in 1841, and finally presented to the college library in 1854 (Marvin L. Colker, *Trinity College, Dublin: Descriptive Catalogue of the Medieval and Renaissance Latin Manuscripts*, ii (1991), pp 1226–38).

After the fall of Napoleon it was only natural that Great Britain should be highly regarded by the papacy. When in 1825 the British minister at Naples, Sir William Hamilton, asked for copies of documents in the Vatican Archives relating to the history of Great Britain and Ireland the request was favourably received. The work was carried out over three years under the supervision of the papal archivist, Marini, and the transcripts were sent to London with the proviso that there be no publication. The collection was lodged in the State Paper Office, London. It consisted of 6,814 documents of a very miscellaneous character dating from 1216 to 1760. In 1842 it was transferred to the library of the British Museum, where it remains as Additional MSS 15351–15401.

By now, however, it was well on the way to being dated. In Rome a young priest, Patrick Francis Moran (1830–1911), became vice-rector of the Irish College in 1856. With the active encouragement of his uncle, Archbishop Paul Cullen of Dublin, he began to search the papal archives for material for Irish

Church history and he found much. At the same time the German priest-historian, Augustin Theiner, was appointed to the staff of the Vatican Archives in 1850, and he became prefect in 1855. The history of the Irish Church was among his wide-ranging interests, and it led to the publication of a large volume of source-material, *Vetera Monuinenta Hibernorum et Scotorum* (Rome, 1864). Meantime in London the Public Record Office had grown into a scholarly institution, with a role in the development of historical studies, rather than being simply a repository for documents no longer administratively current. In the discharge of this new role it was anxious to search in archives abroad, and a proposal for the Vatican Archives was tabled in 1866. Various influential Catholic ecclesiastics offered their help – Bishop Ullathorne of Birmingham, Patrick Francis Moran, now in Dublin as secretary to his uncle, just created cardinal, and Charles W. Russell, president of Maynooth. Joseph Stevenson was proposed as the research-worker, and he seemed well fitted for the job. He had worked in the Public Record Office on the Calendars of State Papers. He had become a convert to Catholicism and had been ordained a priest. However, a less favourable atmosphere was developing in Rome, signalled by Pope Pius IX's 'Syllabus of Condemned Errors' in 1864, and in 1870 Theiner was dismissed from his post because he had leaked documentation to the anti-infallibilist group at the Vatican Council.

Nevertheless, Stevenson, who arrived in Rome in 1872, was for a time given an extraordinarily almost unlimited access to the archives. There were, of course, problems – very limited opening hours, difficulties in getting copies, and, most of all, the fact that in 1872 he was sixty-eight years of age. He retired a little more than four years later, aged seventy-two. His work is classified as 31/9 in the Public Record Office. The successor chosen was William H. Bliss of the Bodleian Library. There were difficulties with the Vatican, not helped by the fact that Bliss himself was a difficult person, but they were overcome through the influence of Cardinal Cullen and Charles W. Russell. Then the whole Roman scene changed in 1878, with the death of Pope Pius IX and the election of Leo XIII. In 1881 the new pope opened the Vatican Archives to duly accredited scholars. Soon material was coming back to London in considerable quantity, amounting in the end to 170 volumes (P.R.O., 31/10).

The Public Record Office was coming under pressure to publish calendars of this material. The pressure came from the Treasury, anxious to see tangible justification for the public money expended. Bliss was very unwilling, conscious of the difficulty of the material, but the pressure was relentless and a calendar covering the years 1198 to 1304 appeared in 1894. For many reasons it had many faults, but it did not deserve the vicious notices it received from Rev Bartholomew McCarthy in the *Irish Ecclesiastical Record* in 1895 and 1896, followed up by attacks by Maurice Healy in parliament for this waste of public money. (Ironically, McCarthy himself suffered a similar offensive review of his edition of the Annals of Ulster from Whitley Stokes in the *Revue Celtique* (Jan. 1897).

But research and publication went on. J.A. Twemlow was appointed assistant to Bliss in 1896, and when Bliss died in 1909 J.M. Rigg was appointed in his place. Twemlow continued to work on the medieval registers, but Rigg turned to the sixteenth century, which was seen as falling into the class of 'state paper' material, a reasonable categorisation, for with the papacy as with Tudor England there had been a great development of the secretariate. But because of diminished resources after the first World War the decision had to be taken to end research in foreign archives. The published fruit of that research was, firstly, fourteen volumes of papal letters, though volumes xiii and xiv were available only in sheets and unindexed. They covered the years 1198 to 1492. Secondly, there was the one volume of petitions, published in 1897, and covering the years 1342 to 1419. Finally, J.M. Rigg's work was represented by two volumes, *State Papers relating to English affairs in the Vatican Archives and Library* (1916, 1926), covering the years 1558 to 1578. The manuscripts of Bliss, Twemlow and Rigg are in P.R.O., 31/10.

The project revived under the auspices of the Irish Manuscripts Commission. This body had been set up in October 1928, with a wide brief to report on manuscripts relating to Ireland and to arrange for and supervise programmes of publication. It was natural that the Vatican Archives should come into the sights of the Commission, and that there should be talk of continuing the series. There were false starts, but these at least led to the indexing and publication of volumes xiii (1955) and xiv (1961). What really allowed the series to get under way was a project of the dynamic director of the National Library of Ireland, Richard Hayes. This was to microfilm and collect for the Library all documents relating to Ireland. It was vast in its conception, and very extensive indeed in its execution, as will be clear from the massive *Guide to the Sources for Irish Civilisation* (11 vols, Boston, 1965); *First Supplement 1965–75* (3 vols, Boston, 1979). This provided the microfilm for the calendar of papal letters. The Public Record Office in London was unwilling to become involved, but the Irish Manuscripts Commission secured a post for an editor, and the British Academy has made an annual grant for the services of a second one. Under the general editorship of Leonard E. Boyle, OP, (ob. 19 Oct. 1999), then Professor of Palaeography and Diplomatic at the Pontifical Institute of Medieval Studies at the University of Toronto and later Prefect of the Vatican Library, five volumes have been added, bringing the material covered down to 1513. These later volumes are of a decidedly higher standard of scholarship than the earlier ones. Researchers are particularly directed to the long introductions to volume xv: 'The papal Chancery at the end of the fifteenth century' by Leonard E. Boyle, and 'Content and method of the Calendar and notes on the formulary and the schedules' by Michael J. Haren, editor of the volume.

The topics dealt with in the papal letters are very varied. The main categories are marriage dispensations, indulgences and collation to benefices, this last one being by far the largest, and increasingly so. Particularly in this context regret is sometimes expressed that the calendar of petitions never got beyond one volume, but the loss is hardly great, and it would be hard to find justification for detailed calendars of both series. The papal 'letter' is normally a response to a 'petition'. In the matter of a benefice, the reply will normally recite the facts as set out in the petition, and appoint judges delegate to examine the alleged facts and either grant or reject it. When the benefice was granted there was a tax to pay, the 'annates' or 'first fruits', first imposed on parish benefices by Pope John XXII (1316–34). The names 'annates' and 'first fruits' might suggest that the amount to be paid was the first year's revenue, but in fact it amounted to half this at most, and less for poorer benefices. The poorest of all, worth less than about six marks (£4) a year, were exempt, and many Irish benefices were of this kind. But where tax was due the beneficiary had to give a written undertaking to pay it (the 'annate bond'). This bond was sometimes signed even when no tax was due 'free because he is poor', 'free because he is an Irishman and poor', and even 'free because he is Irish'.

The earliest Irish annate bond is dated 1420, and they continue into the 1530s. They were transcribed from the registers by Michael Costello, OP (1824–1906). He was posted to Rome in 1867, and soon total deafness isolated a naturally reclusive person. In 1900 the firm of Tempest of Dundalk agreed to publish the work, but things went slowly. The first – and, as it turned out, the only – volume appeared in 1912, with an introduction by Ambrose Coleman, OP: *De Annatis Hiberniae. Volume I: Ulster*. It carried the imprint of M.H. Gill and Son of Dublin and the 'Record Society, St Patrick's College, Maynooth'. This was the newly-founded Catholic Record Society of Ireland. The Society also purchased the transcripts of the annates for the other three ecclesiastical provinces. Those for the dioceses of Dublin and Kildare appeared as a supplement to the Society's journal, *Archivium Hibernicum*, ii (1913). Publication of the annates resumed in volume x (1943) and was completed (except for the diocese of Leighlin) in volume xxix (1970).

From what has been said it will be clear that what has been published from the pre-Reformation Vatican Archives contains much information about individual Irish people, most of them unknown from any other source. In the nature of things, most of them are clergy, but there are laity. Particularly in regard to the collation of benefices it must always be borne in mind that the 'papal letter' does not set out facts but is a judicial mandate ordering an investigation as to whether the facts recited are true. It must be remembered too that there is still much unexplored material (Michael J. Haren, 'Vatican Archives as a historical source to *c*.1530' in *Archivium Hibernicum*, xxxix (1984)). But though it has been picked over to some extent, what has been published still contains rich pickings for the local historian if carefully used, especially in establishing lists of the parish clergy for the fourteenth and fifteenth centuries. The papal registers are in a calendar in English which, certainly in the later volumes, may be regarded as good enough to make it unnecessary to consult the originals. This is just as well, for the hand in the later registers is very difficult indeed. The annate-bonds have been edited in a full Latin text, but they are well annotated and they follow the same simple formula with only a couple of variations, so that they should present little difficulty even to the almost completely Latinless.

III. IRISH INITIATIVES AND THE VATICAN ARCHIVES

At this stage it will be useful to list some developments that have played a major role in exploring Irish material in the Vatican Archives. The Irish Manuscripts Commission and the programme of microfilming in the National Library have been mentioned. The Catholic Record Society of Ireland, also mentioned above, arose from debates at the meeting of the Maynooth Union in 1910 and 1911. Its declared purpose was to collect and publish documents, 'more especially those documents which have some bearing on Irish ecclesiastical history'. Its journal, *Archivium Hibernicum*, first appeared in 1912, and apart from the gap between volumes vii (1921) and viii (1941) has been reasonably faithful to its professed aim of being an annual publication. In 1945 the Irish Franciscans set up a House of Studies in Killiney. From here there came in 1958 the first volume of a periodical, *Collectanea Hibernica*, subtitled 'Sources for Irish History', likewise an annual publication, and perhaps a little more faithful than *Archivium Hibernicum* in this respect. In October 1957 the Irish Catholic Historical Committee was set up on the initiative of the late Professor R. Dudley Edwards of University College, Dublin. At its first meeting it adopted a far-reaching programme, but what developed was the holding of a conference once a year. There have been difficulties in having the papers of this conference published, but by and large they have been – from 1955 to 1961 under the title *Proceedings of the Irish Catholic Historical Committee*, from 1962 to 1968 in the *Irish Ecclesiastical Record*, and, after a brief hiatus, in *Archivium Hibernicum* since 1973. The papers published in the Irish Ecclesiastical Record were reprinted in five fascimiles, entitled *Proceedings of the Irish Catholic Historical Committee 1962* (Dublin, 1963), *1963* (1965), *1964* (1967), *1965–1967* (1968) and *1968* (1969). Reflecting the dominant interest of Professor Edwards, the series includes a number of valuable short reports on archives.

All these initiatives concerned themselves with Irish historical material in the papal archives, especially post-Reformation material. Like all other administrations, the papal curia became more complex from the sixteenth century onwards. The old expediting offices, especially the Datary, which had generated so much of the material in the 'papal letters', declined in importance. By contrast, the secretariate grew in importance – indeed it was already moving in on the Datary's functions well before the Reformation. Now its competence expanded, especially through the growth of nunciatures. New nunciatures were set up and they and the older nunciatures were consciously developed as instruments of religious reform. This process was well established by the pontificate of Gregory XIII (1572–85). The increasing business of the Roman-directed reform had led to specific tasks being regularly committed to commissions of cardinals. Some of these commissions were of their nature permanent, the Inquisition, for example. In 1588 Pope Sixtus V set up fifteen permanent 'congregations', six of them concerned with the government of the papal states and nine with the religious affairs of the universal Church. The missions were still a great exception to this Roman centralism, being enmeshed especially in the claims of Portugal and Spain. In 1622 Pope Gregory XV set up a congregation to deal specifically with the missions, colloquially known as 'Propaganda' down the centuries, from its Latin title, 'Congregatio de Propaganda Fide'. The thinking of the time included the Protestant-ruled countries of Europe in 'mission territory'. Ireland was included among them, though it was unique in retaining its historic diocesan episcopate. In consequence, routine ecclesiastical business in Rome was transacted with Propaganda until a further change by Pope Pius X in 1908. This removed the by now great anomaly that countries with established hierarchies, not just Ireland but England and even giants like the United States, should be 'mission countries' in canon law. From now on their Roman business would be done, not with Propaganda, but with various other congregations. Finally, it must be borne in mind that the interests of the Holy See in Irish affairs could extend beyond the strictly religious to the diplomatic and even to the political. Documentation under these heads would not end up in the archives of Propaganda but elsewhere in the Vatican.

The main Vatican Archive is understandably a vast and complex affair. Archives are by nature always tending to get out of control, and highly-placed administrators are among the great disturbers of archives. This is shown strikingly in the Vatican by the Borghese and Barberini collections. When Pope Paul V died in 1621 his nephew and secretary of state, Cardinal Scipio Borghese, took with him on leaving office a huge collection of papers, most but not all relating to his uncle's pontificate. The same thing happened on the death of Pope Urban VIII Barberini in 1644. Both collections remained with the Borghese and Barberini families until the former was recovered for the Vatican Archives in 1892 and the latter, slightly anomalously, for the Vatican Library ten years later.

The most recently published guide to this rich complexity is Francis X. Bloum, *Vatican Archives: an Inventory and Guide to Historical Documents of the Holy See* (Oxford, 1997). The first explorers for Irish material were, as has been seen, Theiner and Moran. Moran's principal publication of source material was *Spicilegium Ossoriense* (3 vols, Dublin, 1874–84), the '*Ossoriense*' no doubt commemorating his appointment as bishop in Ossory, and '*spicilegium*', literally 'a gleaning of ears of corn' meant as modestly self-deprecatory. In truth, Moran makes no concessions to those struggling with a foreign language, apart from a table of contents setting out the documents to be presented in Latin or Italian text in chronological order, with no more than a general reference to the archive from which the document was taken. Moran lived a very busy life, and relied on transcripts he had made hurriedly, or more frequently had had others make for him, and in consequence his text is not always totally accurate.

Moran's successor was another vice-rector of the Irish College, Rome, John Hagan. In a series of contributions to the newly-founded *Archivium Hibernicum*, between 1913 and 1921 (vols ii–vii) he published documentation running to about 700 pages under the general title 'Miscellanea Vaticano-Hibernica'. Again, he printed the full text of each document in Latin or Italian, but in almost all cases he provided a summary in English and a precise archive reference, though this will now need checking, for a certain amount of recataloging is always going on. But Hagan introduced Irish Church historians to much detail in the Vatican Archives – the secretariate of State in its nunciature correspondence; the Congregation of the Council with its records of the appointment of bishops and its files of reports on their diocese sent to Rome by these bishops (*relationes status*); and the two great collections, Borghese and Barberini, recently recovered by the Vatican.

For the next generation interest tended to shift to the archives of Propaganda. Here Irish material was more obvious but provision for researchers was made more slowly. (The historical archives of Propaganda are not part of the general Vatican archives, but remain in the Congregation's administrative headquarters.) Interest returned to the main Vatican Archive with the microfilming programme of Dr Richard Hayes of the National Library, for the very practical reason that there were no microfilm facilities at Propaganda. Irish scholars were sent to the Vatican to examine, report, and order film for the library. Cathaldus Giblin, OFM, examined the Flanders nunciature. This was important because during the seventeenth and eighteenth centuries the Holy See transacted routine business concerning the affairs of the British Isles through the nuncio in Brussels. (It should be noted that the nuncio had two principal correspondents in Rome, the cardinal secretary of state and the cardinal prefect of Propaganda, and only the first of these is filed in the nunciature series in the Vatican.) He presented a preliminary report in a paper to the Irish Catholic Historical Committee in 1956. He followed this with an extremely detailed calendar extending over eleven numbers of *Collectanea Hibernica* (i, iii–v, ix–xv) of a two-way correspondence dating from 1552 to 1790. It is always risky to say of a calendar that it is so good that you may dispense with the original, but in this case it is a very reasonable risk.

P.E. MacFhinn did a similar exploration of the so-called 'English nunciature', 'Nunziatura d'Inghilterra'. His guide, entitled 'Scríbhinní i gCartlainn an Vatican: Tuarascbháil' was published in the journal of the Irish Manuscripts

Commission, *Analecta Hibernica*, xvi (1946). There never was an 'English nunciature', of course, and this collection was put together for archival purposes. In the nature of things it contains much Irish material. The report is idiosyncratic, switching between three languages, Irish, Latin and Italian, and ranging from full texts to brief one-line notices. There is an index in *Analecta Hibernica*, xix (1957).

Cathaldus Giblin was also responsible for a detailed examination of the Barberini papers, resulting in more microfilm and a catalogue: 'Vatican Library: MSS Barberini Latini' in *Archivium Hibernicum*, xviii (1955), giving a brief summary of every document relating to Ireland. Dominic Conway worked on the even larger Borghese collection ('Guide to documents of Irish and British interest in the Fondo Borghese' in *Archivium Hibernicum*, xxiii (1960), xxiv (1961).

At the beginning of the century Nicholas Donnelly had published from the *Per obitum* volumes in the Vatican Archives (*Archivium Hibernicum*, i (1912)) records of appointments of priests in the diocese of Dublin between 1594 and 1687. These appear to be from the records of the Datary. The continuing activity of the Datary in the Church of the Counter-reformation appears also from Cathaldus Giblin, 'The Processus Datariae and the appointment of Irish bishops in the seventeenth century', published in the tercenerary volume, *Father Luke Wadding* (Dublin, 1957). The processes are a series of inquiries into the suitability of candidates for the episcopate, dating from 1623 to 1697. These inquiries were normally carried out by the Consistorial Congregation, but were seemingly entrusted to the Datary when the inquiry could not be carried out in the candidate's diocese, as was normally the case for Ireland.

Other promising collections have been explored as part of the same programme. In 1963 Giblin reported to the Irish Catholic Historical Committee on 'Material relating to Ireland in the *Albani* collection of MSS in the Vatican Archives'. This collection of 265 volumes deals with the pontificate of Clement XI Albani. It covers the years 1690 to 1721 and may be taken in conjunction with the Stuart papers at Windsor. In 1971 he reported (*Archivium Hibernicum*, xxvi) on 'Vatican Archives: lettere di Particolari', 313 volumes of assorted correspondence dating from 1578 to 1803. Years earlier F.M. Jones, C SS R, had published from this source (*Archivium Hibernicum*, xvii (1953) the full text of 'Correspondence of Father Ludovico Mansoni, SJ, papal nuncio to Ireland', thirteen letters dating from 1601 and 1602. In 1995 Hugh Fenning, OP, reported (*Archivium Hibernicum*, xlix) on 'Documents of Irish interest in the *Fondo Missioni* of the Vatican Archives'. The origins of this collection are obscure: it may be Propaganda material gone astray when the French loot was returned after the downfall of Napoleon. In any case, it yielded 218 documents of Irish interest, mainly of the eighteenth century.

By the first quarter of the seventeenth century Ireland had taken a decision without parallel in Catholic Europe, in that the great majority of the people had refused to follow the religion of their civil ruler, though this ruler was otherwise broadly acceptable; and as the sixteenth-century conflicts died down it became possible to maintain a Catholic episcopate in the historic Irish sees. In 1622 the Congregation of Propaganda was founded and from then until 1908 all routine Irish Catholic religious business was transacted through Propaganda. The Congregation moved to what is still its headquarters in 1667, the baroque Collegio di Propaganda Fide just off the Piazza di Spagna, and when its archives began to pass from the administrative to the historical they were not deposited in the general Vatican Archives but remained in the administrative headquarters. One consequence of this was that when Pope Leo XIII opened the Vatican Archives in 1881 Propaganda was slower to provide such things as inventories and copying facilities. All this ground has now been made up, and it is a pleasure to work in this small and informal archive.

The basic introduction to the holdings is the *Inventory of the Historical Archives*, the work of two successive archivists, Nicholas Kowalsky and Josef Metzler (Rome, 1983, bilingual English/Italian text). A brief report to the Irish Catholic Historical Committee in 1956 by Benignus Millett, OFM, 'The archives of the Congregation de Propaganda Fide', includes some useful practical hints based on his own extensive experience. And the walls of the reading-room are lined with the administrative inventories built up over the centuries, so that finding one's way is very easy once there is an understanding of how the Congregation went about its business.

Like all Roman congregations, Propaganda was made up of a Cardinal Prefect, a number of assistant cardinals (who would also have responsibilities in other branches of the administration), together with a secretary and a small office staff. Every month there was a general meeting of all the cardinals, with the secretary. This was known as a *congregazione generale*. Proceedings were formal, with an agenda and minutes, the *Acta*, in Italian, *Atti*. These minutes were later bound in chronological order and indexed, not very lavishly, it must be admitted. As each item on the agenda cane up the bundle of documents relating to it was on the table. For the nineteenth century the more important of these documents were normally circulated in printed form together with the agenda and incorporated in the minutes. The tabled documents were later carefully bound in the order in which they had been tabled, in a series known as *Scritture riferite nelle Congregazioni Generali*. There is no index to this important collection, and it has been known for researchers to go a long time without being aware of its existence. As should be clear from a knowledge of how the Congregation worked, the *Acta* are the index to the *Scritture*. It must be noted, however, that from 1622 to 1668 this tidy scheme does not exist. The 417 volumes of the *Scritture* for these years are not in good order, but they have been so much worked over that it is now well known where material dealing with various countries is to be found (see the list in *Inventory*

S. Charles' Day

My Dear Dr Kirby

I wrote a few lines ere yesterday and continue my correspondence to day. The Maynooth commission has adjourned its proceedings until Christmas. They have examined every thing and every one most minutely. They made some of the students spell & read English — and were so little satisfied with their proficiency, that in their last list of questions they ask "would it not be desirable to employ a national schoolmaster to teach spelling and reading to the students". I mention this because I dare say it is be most useful to examine your own students on the same matters. I recollect some who c^d not spell a word. You c^d easily try them by dictating a piece of English and making them copy it as you w^d read. It w^d be also of great importance to teach the students to read slowly and distinctly. It is impossible to be heard in a large church unless the reading be slow and distinct. A little declamation

1. Archbishop Paul Cullen to Tobias Kirby, rector of the Irish College, Rome, 4 November 1855 (Irish College, Rome: Kirby papers, Add MSS 1/2/106)

of the Historical Archives, pp 29–39). It might be further noted that some of the Propaganda Archives were mistakenly sent to Vienna after the fall of Napoleon. They were recovered by the Congregation only in 1925. They are still shelved separately under the title 'Fondo di Vienna'. Four volumes contain Irish material dating between 1653 and 1668.

The monthly meeting would normally reach a decision on matters before it, and this would normally involve the writing of a letter or letters. These were registered in a series of letter-books, the *Lettere*. Where there were matters of special difficulty a subcommittee (*congregazione particolare*) might be set up. Its deliberations are filed in a separate series, running to 161 volumes. There is Irish material in nineteen of them, ranging from 1668 to 1860. At the other end of the scale were matters considered too routine or too trivial to be referred to the full meeting of cardinals, though they can often be of more interest to the historian than ecclesiastically weightier matters. These were dealt with at a weekly meeting (*congresso*) of the Cardinal Prefect and the secretary to review the week's post, at which they took decisions on routine matters. Though these decisions would normally involve writing a letter, such letters were not registered, and a scribbled archival note is often the only clue to what had been decided. However, the documents on which the decision was taken were carefully preserved, and later bound in geographical and chronological order. There are in all forty-five volumes of solidly Irish material in these *Scritture riferite nei Congressi*, ranging from 1625 to 1892 and they are a real treasure house. As well, there are a number of smaller series which can contain Irish documents. They are described in the *Inventory of the Historical Archives*.

This simple and logical method of filing material was supplanted by a totally new method in 1893. It is set out succinctly in the *Inventory of the Historical Archives*, pp 85–90. Shortly afterwards, in 1908, Ireland and several other countries were removed from the 'missionary' care of Propaganda and from then on their business was divided between the other congregations.

Up to about a generation ago the researcher in Propaganda could make a precis of his document, copy it laboriously by hand, or have a typed copy made by the archive attendant, for whom this work probably represented a substantial part of his earnings. The great Irish researcher of this 'heroic age' was undoubtedly Brendan Jennings, OFM. His work is to be found in many places, the Propaganda material especially over many issues of *Archivium Hibernicum* in the 1940s and 1950s. It was in the tradition of Theiner and Moran, full texts in Latin or Italian with minimum concession to the monoglot. His successor in what might be called the 'microfilm age' is his fellow-Franciscan, Benignus Millett. The National Library has done a great deal of microfilming in the Propaganda Archives, especially the *Congressi* series, where whole volumes of Irish material presented themselves. Against the background of this microfilm conveniently available in Dublin Benignus Millett has concentrated on brief calendars, most if not all of seventeenth-century material, which he publishes in *Collectanea Hibernica*, with precise reference to both the archive location and the microfilm. He has been the general editor of *Collectanea Hibernica* since its foundation, and for years past it is the exceptional number of the periodical that is without a substantial contribution from him.

IV. COLLEGES AND RELIGIOUS HOUSES

Needless to say, there is more to Rome than the papal archives. The records of the Roman vicariate list many Irish students ordained in the city. A list has recently been published covering the 'Stuart years' (Hugh Fenning, OP, 'Irishmen ordained at Rome 1698–1759' in *Archivium Hibernicum*, i (1996)). Rather less than might be expected came from the Irish College for diocesan priests. Founded in 1628, it very quickly passed into the control of mainly Italian Jesuits, and remained a small institution. John Hanly gave a survey of its records in a report to the Irish Catholic Historical Committee in 1963 ('Sources for the history of the Irish College, Rome') and the following year he published résumés of the oaths taken at entry by 142 students between 1633 and 1773, which in some cases have family and topographical detail ('Records of the Irish College, Rome, under Jesuit administration' in *Archivium Hibernicum*, xxvii (1964)). The college really came into its own when it reopened under Irish diocesan priests in 1826, twenty-eight years after it had been closed in the disturbances of the French occupation of Rome and the papal states. Until the appointment of a papal nuncio to Ireland in 1930 the rector of the Irish College was in practice the intermediary between most Irish bishops and the Holy See. The volume of this business increased enormously with the development of communications in the nineteenth century (see Patrick J. Corish, 'Irish College, Rome: Kirby Papers' in *Archivium Hibernicum*, xxx–xxxii (1972–4)).

The religious orders maintained a strong presence in Rome since the Counter-reformation, the friars in particular establishing their own Irish houses. As well, the archives of their generalates contain much Irish material. Those of the Jesuit generalate in Borgo S. Spirito would appear to be particularly rich. The following can be recommended as introductions to the archival holdings of the specifically Irish houses and of the respective generalates: F.X. Martin, OSA, 'Archives of the Irish Augustinians, Rome: a summary Report' in *Archivium Hibernicum*, xviii (1955) and F.X. Martin, OSA and A. de Meijer, OSA, 'Irish Material in the Augustinian General Archives, Rome', ibid., xix (1956); Conleth Kearns, OP, 'Archives of the Irish College, San Clemente, Rome: a summary Report', ibid., xviii (1955) and Hugh Fenning, OP, 'Irish material in the Registers of the Dominican Masters General, 1390–1649' in *Archivum Fratrum Praedicatorum*, xxxix (1969); Benignus Millett, OFM, 'The archives of St Isidore's College, Rome' (a summary report to the Irish Catholic Historical Committee) in *Archivium Hibernicum*, xl (1985), Brendan Jennings, OFM, 'Documents from the archives of St Isidore's College, Rome' in *Analecta Hibernica* vi (1934) and Patrick Conlan OFM, 'A short-title catalogue of *Hibernia* ... in the General Archives of the Friars Minor, Rome' in *Collectanea Hibernica*, xviii–xix (1976–7) and xx (1978) to xxvii–xxviii (1985–6) and xxxiv–xxxv (1992–3). The overall limiting dates are 1706 to 1900, with the bulk of the material between 1870 and 1900.

Rome was not the only place where the Irish left their traces in Europe, especially during the seventeenth and eighteenth centuries, when 'soldiers, scholars, priests' were to be found all over the continent. Attention might be called to two good overall guides: for the sixteenth and seventeenth centuries John J. Silke, 'The Irish abroad in the age of the Counter-reformation 1534–1691' in *A New History of Ireland*, iii (1976), 587–633 (with a useful map), and for the eighteenth century Cathaldus Giblin, OFM, 'Irish Exiles in Catholic Europe' in Corish, *Ir. Catholicism*, iv, 3 (1971).

A glance at John Silke's map will immediately suggest that no fully comprehensive survey of all the sites is possible. Beyond question much still awaits unearthing in many places: for example, the discoveries of Benignus Millett recently in the state archives in Prague ('Some lists of Irish Franciscans in Prague 1651–1791' in *Collectanea Hibernica*, xxxvi–xxxvii (1994–5)). Because of the Penal Laws it was not possible to set up in Ireland houses of formation which the Council of Trent had envisaged for the training of the clergy. Soon Irish houses began to dot the map of Catholic Europe.

Most of them were small, many of them had slender financial resources, and in consequence some came and went. But those that established themselves were rather more than houses of clerical formation, at least those of them where the Irish managed to keep direction and control. They were centres for the Irish community in exile, places where people met to exchange information and reminiscence. This situation changed completely after the system had been to a great extent swept away by the French Revolution. Only three seminaries for diocesan priests were re-established – Rome, Paris and Salamanca – and of these both Paris and Salamanca had little dealing with the wider world outside the seminary.

On the eve of the French Revolution the Irish seminary presence was concentrated in France, with two-thirds of the total places. Of these, 180 were in two colleges in Paris – over half the French total. An Irish seminary presence in Paris dated back to 1578. It had found a permanent home in the Collège des Lombards in 1677. During the eighteenth century it became increasingly common that young men be already ordained priests before being sent abroad to study theology. Increased tensions between these ordained priests and younger students led to the foundation of a separate college for the students in the Rue du Cheval Vert in 1769. Both institutions were closed by the

2. *Map 1* Irish Colleges abroad

French Revolution, and the Collège des Lombards did not reopen after it. The other college did, thanks to the skill and courage of the Abbé John Baptist Walsh, and the street where it was situated was renamed Rue des Irlandais in 1808. The reopened institution was looked on with disfavour for a time by the Irish Church authorities for a number of reasons. It was not helpful that the adventurer Richard Ferris managed to insinuate himself into the administration of the college. There were more serious issues, however, in that Napoleon was heir to both the Revolution and a kind of neo-Gallicanism, and with Britain and France at war the Irish bishops could not be unmindful of the fact that they owed little to revolutionary France and much to the British government, specifically the small annual grant that kept Maynooth functioning. It had been given with a fair measure of suspicion, but there were no real strings attached.

The Collège des Irlandais functioned as a seminary from 1814 to 1939. It closed at the opening of the second world war, and it did not reopen. Thirty years ago it must have looked as if this Irish institution had no future. That corner would now seem to have been turned, and the college will remain in Irish hands. It had been a great achievement of the Abbé Walsh to have recovered much archival material confiscated by the revolutionary state. This has now been calendared by Liam Swords, 'History of the Irish College, Paris, 1578–1800: Calendar of the papers of the Irish College, Paris' in *Archivium Hibernicum*, xxxv (1980). It is obvious that this does not represent a routine seminary archive, but that Walsh concentrated on recovering documents concerning titles to property or investments (*rentes*). It is also clear that not all the documents concern the institution in the Rue du Cheval Vert, which, it must be remembered, was in existence for only twenty years before the French Revolution. In the nature of things, there is much from the older Collège des Lombards, and some material from other Irish colleges in France, specifically the large seminary at Nantes and the relatively large one at Bordeaux. Overall, there is a good deal of social history for the local historian in these papers now in the Irish College, Paris.

The archives of Paris have been explored for Irish material in a number of studies, such as Ruth Clark, *Strangers and sojourners at Port Royal* (Cambridge, 1932) and Thomas O'Connor, *An Irish Theologian in Enlightenment France* (Dublin, 1995). What is very clear is that there is a great deal still to be found, as may be seen from the fascinating discovery published by Liam Swords in 'Calendar of Irish materials in the files of Jean Fromont, notary at Paris May 1701–24 Jan. 1730' in *Collectanea Hibernica*, xxxiv–xxxv (1992–3), xxxvi–xxxvii (1994–5). Fromont was the notary dealing with the business of the Irish College and also with that of many of the Irish in Paris.

Attention might also be directed to the brief report made to the Irish Catholic Historical Committee in 1955 by T.J. Walsh, 'Archives in France as a source of Irish history', which at least opens up possibilities in many directions. His book, *The Irish Continental College Movement* (Dublin and Cork, 1973) deals with Bordeaux, Toulouse and Lille. The confiscations of the French Revolution swept the archives of many ecclesiastical institutions into local archives, usually those of the département. The buildings of the college at Bordeaux, a Munster stronghold, with forty places in 1789, are still intact, but used as a garage. A French priest, the Abbé Jean-Baptiste Pelette, trawled the Archives départmentales de la Gironde and the municipal archives of Bordeaux for surviving records (T.J. Walsh, 'Some records of the Irish College at Bordeaux' in *Archivium Hibernicum*, xv (1950)). What he recovered concerning the college was fragmentary, but there was much on Irish priests ordained at Bordeaux who did not return to Ireland but served out their lives in the Gironde. Toulouse, also a Munster stronghold, was small college, with twelve places in 1789. What survives of its records was extracted from the Archives Départmentales de la Haute Garonne in Toulouse by Patrick Boyle ('The Irish seminary at Toulouse' in *Archivium Hibernicum*, i (1912)). It is a miscellaneous collection stretching from the foundation of the college in 1659 to its confiscation in 1793, with names of students and college officials. There are admission lists, with details of family background and place of origin, for just a single decade, 1684–94.

The Catholic Netherlands, Spanish in the seventeenth century and Austrian in the eighteenth, provided a culture where Irish institutions could flourish. Two of the colleges founded there, Douai with thirty places in 1789 and Lille

Joanes wadingus diocesis Fernensis ortus in oppido wexfordiæ, pa-
rentibus Gualtero wadingo, et Margarita walsh ejusdem oppidi catholicis
& legitimo matrimonio iunctis. Prioris rudimentis studuit wexfordiæ
magistris Nicolao Quifero, et Jacobo Denerox catholicis et Gualtero Faus
Grammatica Rossiæ magistro Philippo keatting catholico. Hispaniam appulit
Amantiæ erat apud D. Thō strong episcopo ossoriensi sitiant? plus minus Co-
postella? visitatione inde se contulit, ubi in numero collegarum admissus
humanioribus literis incubuit anō et dimidio; pro ejusdem collegij pro-
curanda quæstione in curia cū Rectore psectus e; morbi deinde gra-
vitate coactus patriam repetijt, qua recuperata Deo cū abijt vō? in
numero et collegarum cooptatz, ubi et Rhethoricæ et logicæ studuit
per annū ghiquinū, et pro collegij illius juvanda utilitate et quæstione
in Hispania cū D. Davidi Rothæo ejusdē collegij præfecto ad curiam
Philippi accessit, et pacto feliciter negotio ejusdē Dn. Davidis impetra-
tione in hoc Hibernorum seminariū salmā xa norma regulam rite
examinatus admissus ē a Rectore P. Thō biko de societate Jesu, ætati-
suæ anō 23 plusminus die 18 octobris ann 1601.

with eight, had been conquered by France in 1667, and presumably suffered the fate of French institutions in 1793. Brendan Jennings, OFM, has published material about them from the Propaganda archives in Rome, 'Reports on Irish colleges in the Low Countries' in *Archivium Hibernicum*, xvi (1951); and also 'Documents of the Irish College at Douai', ibid., x (1943) which, curiously enough, have ended up in the Archives Générales du Royaume in Brussels. An exploration of the Archives Départmentales du Nord at Lille or the municipal archives at Douai might be worthwhile.

The college at Antwerp, founded in 1600, still offered thirty places in 1789. Up to recently little was known about it, but it has now been shown how much can be extracted from local archives, in this case those of the city and diocese of Antwerp. These have produced detailed records of the college, with contemporary maps and sketches of buildings, and records of 286 students of the college who received orders (Jeroen Nilis, 'The Irish College Antwerp' in *Clogher Record*, xv, 3 (1996)).

The great clustering of Irish was, however, in Louvain, the academic centre of the Catholic Netherlands. Its matriculation registers have yielded the names of Irish students from the time they began to seek out Louvain in preference to Oxford to the suppression in the 1790s (Brendan Jennings, OFM, 'The Irish students in the University of Louvain, 1584–1794' in *Measgra Mhichíl Uí Chléirigh* (Dublin, 1944)). The records of two of them seem to have been lost the Pastoral College for diocesan priests and the Dominican College of the Holy Cross – that is, unless something turns up from the Archives Générales du Royaume or the Bibliothèque Royale. Those of the third, and most famous, had a happier if adventurous outcome. The Irish Franciscan College of St Anthony had been founded in 1606. It was suppressed in the French Revolution, but the Franciscans recovered it as a House of Studies in 1925, and still maintain a presence there. A very substantial part of the archives was taken to St Isidore's in Rome in the 1790s, and from there to Ireland after 1870, when the threat of confiscation arose in Italy (see Brendan Jennings, OFM (ed.), *Louvain Papers 1606–1827* (Dublin, 1968)). However, some Louvain Franciscan papers ended in Belgian repositories, and no more than a beginning has been made with locating and publishing them (A.A. Wijffels, 'Calendar of documents relating to St Anthony's College, Louvain' in *Collectanea Hibernica*, xxiv (1982)).

Louvain was situated in the great diocese of Mechelen (Malines) and as might be expected the diocesan archives have extensive records of Irishmen ordained to the priesthood or licensed as preachers or confessors (Brendan Jennings, OFM, 'Irish names in the Malines Ordination Registers, 1607–1794' in *Irish Ecclesiastical Record*, 5th series, nine contributions between lxxv (1951) and lxvii (1952), and 'Irish preachers and confessors in the archdiocese of Malines, 1607–1794' in *Archivium Hibernicum*, xxiii (1960)). The provincial record of religious orders can also be rewarding for this country with so large an Irish presence. Some of them were confiscated during the revolutionary years and ended up in state repositories, but the Orders still have substantial holdings. The best-known are those of the Irish Franciscans at Sint-Truiden (Brendan Jennings, OFM, 'Sint-Truiden: Irish Franciscan Documents' in *Archivium Hibernicum*, xxiv–xxvi (1961–3)). The Jesuit provincial archives at Heverlee are also known to contain material of Irish interest.

The Iberian peninsula was never fully subjugated by the French during the Revolution. In the nature of things it had given hospitality to many Irish refugees between the sixteenth and eighteenth centuries. Two brief reports presented to the Irish Catholic Historical Committee in 1955 will serve as an introduction to the records they left behind them – Canice Mooney, OFM, 'The archives of Simancas as a source for Irish ecclesiastical history' and Joseph Ranson, 'Irish archives in Spain'. There had been seven Irish seminaries in Spain, but in 1789 only one remained, Salamanca, with thirty-two places. It had been the largest and most stable in a group where most were small and existed precariously. All except Salamanca had fallen under the control of Spanish Jesuits and were closed when the Jesuits were suppressed in 1767. What of their archives was saved went to Salamanca. Salamanca was also under Jesuit control, but for the most part the superiors were Irish Jesuits, and the college continued to function under Irish diocesan priests, right down to the outbreak of the Spanish Civil War in 1936. It has not been reopened, and the whole archive was transferred to Maynooth. There is still much to be done with it, but it is at least open to researchers.

There has been a certain amount of publication over the years. The rector, Denis J. Doherty, published the list of students who took the admission oaths between 1595 and 1778 (*Archivium Hibernicum*, ii–iv (1913–15)). The earlier ones are very detailed, and full of fascinating social history on family background, place of origin, and previous education. Then, however, the formula became standardised and all that remains is a list of names. Strangely, no official student lists were kept in the nineteenth century, and Doherty had to try to reconstruct them from such things as account-books and university records (*Archivium Hibernicum*, vi (1917)). (The university became a secular institution in 1845, no longer attended by seminarians.) From the university records Amalio Huarte has published documentation on the Irish presence in Salamanca even before an Irish college was founded (*Archivium Hibernicum*, iv (1915), vi (1917)), while the flavour of the college as a clearing house in the mid-eighteenth century for Irish news may be caught in Patrick J. Corish, 'Correspondence of the superiors of the Jesuit mission in Ireland with John O'Brien, SJ, rector of Salamanca' in *Archivium Hibernicum*, xxvii (1964). John J. Silke has shown how much may be collected locally on an Irish college apart from the archival remains that ended up in Salamanca ('The Irish College, Seville' in *Archivium Hibernicum*, xxiv (1961)) and Patricia O'Connell has rescued two other colleges from oblivion ('The Irish College, Santiago de Compostella 1605–1767' in *Archivium Hibernicum*, i (1906) and *The Irish College* at *Alcalá de Henares 1649–1785* (Dublin, 1997). There-were three Irish foundations in Lisbon, of Dominican friars and Dominican nuns, and a seminary for diocesan clergy. The nuns remain, and the friars still minister in the church of Corpo Santo. The seminary, founded in 1593, was closed when the Jesuits were expelled in 1759, but managed to reopen under diocesan clergy in 1782. It was a small institution, offering twelve places in 1789, and it did not survive the liberal regime installed in Portugal as a result of the civil war that broke out in 1820. Little work has been done on these Lisbon records. M. Gonçalves da Costa, *Fontes inéditas Portuguesas para a História de Irlanda* (Braga, 1981) is a useful introduction. It is to be presumed that much was destroyed in the great earthquake of 1755. Hugh Fenning, OP, has published invaluable lists of ordinations of Irish priests between 1660 and 1850 from the archiepiscopal archives in Lisbon (*Collectanea Hibernica*, xxxiv-xxxv (1972–3), xxxvi–xxxvii (1994–5)).

V. LITERARY WORKS, PRINTED AND UNPRINTED

Finally, though they are not strictly archival, it may be worth calling attention to the fact that the Irish exiles in Europe produced much in the form of printed books that are a vital source of Irish Catholic history of the Counter-reformation. Most of them were in Latin, still the basic language of scholarship, though some re-edited in more recent times have the mercy of an English translation. Good general guides are to be found in Benignus Millett, OFM, 'Irish literature in Latin 1550–1700' in *A New History of Ireland*, iii (1976), 561–86 and Michael Walsh, 'Irish books printed abroad 1475–1700' in *The Irish Book*, ii (1963), 1–36. Any list given here must be highly selective. The first to be mentioned must be two works so lengthy that they remained in manuscript, and first saw light under the aegis of the Irish Manuscripts Commission. The massive account of Rinuccini's mission to Ireland as papal nuncio in the 1640s, compiled from his now lost papers by two Irish Capuchins, was published under the title *Commentarius Rinuccinianus* in six volumes between 1932 and 1949, edited by Stanislaus Kavanagh, OFMCap; and the account of the Irish bishops completed in exile by John Lynch in 1672 and edited by John F. O'Doherty (*De Praesulibus Hiberniae*, 2 vols, Dublin, 1944). Of the printed books the following are very useful: David Rothe, *Analecta Sacra* (Cologne 1617–19, edited by Patrick F. Moran, Dublin, 1884); Philip O'Sullivan Beare, *Historiae Catholicae Iberniae Compendium* (Lisbon, 1621, edited by Matthew Kelly, Dublin 1850); Dominic O'Daly, *Initium, incrementa et exitus familiae Ceraldinorum* (Lisbon, 1655, English translation by C.P. Meehan, *The Rise, Increase and Exit of the Geraldines* (Dublin, 1850); John O'Heyne, *Epilogus chronologicus . . . Ordinis Praedicatorum* (Louvain, 1706, edited with an English translation by Ambrose Coleman, OP, Dundalk, 1902); and Thomas Burke, OP, *Hibernia Dominicana* (Kilkenny, 1762). The imprint on this book said 'Cologne', but it was published in Kilkenny, a sign perhaps of changing times, or at least their beginning.

VI. A FEW WORDS TO THE EXPLORER

The real change came however with the French Revolution. It might have seemed in 1815 that the Revolution had been defeated, but in fact the face of Europe was permanently changed. In Ireland too Irish Catholics were beginning to make their way into the political and public life of their country. The exile of the future, predominantly but not exclusively from among the poor, would turn to the opportunities offered by the English-speaking world, especially Britain and the United States. This began another story of Irish Catholicism, but it is not the same kind of story as that of the centuries before the Revolution. Irish Catholics kept their links with the Holy See naturally, and indeed even strengthened them, and in this context the Irish College in Rome was important. But only two other colleges reopened, at Paris and Salamanca, and they tended to become Irish enclaves to a great extent cut off from the surrounding culture.

For more than two centuries, however, from the later sixteenth century to the end of the eighteenth, the sources for much of Irish Catholic culture are to be found in European archives. Much work has been done in them, and much remains to be done. The first step towards future progress is to know what has been done, both to appreciate it in itself and as a guide towards future progress. The next step should be to see how much of the unexplored material exists in copy in Ireland. Here the great source is the National Library microfilm collections, and the principal key to these is the *Guide to the Sources for Irish Civilisation* mentioned earlier. Finally, there is the foreign archive itself. There are very many of them, and they vary so much in character, from small, essentially private, and normally understaffed collections, to large civil or ecclesiastical archives (normally understaffed too). But by the time the relevant archive has been located enough knowledge will have been assembled to at least know where to inquire about the conditions on which it may be consulted. All the repositories discussed here are open to duly recommended historical scholars.

PATRICK J. CORISH

4. Map 2 Catholic Dioceses of Ireland

Records in archives in Ireland

I. DIOCESAN ARCHIVES

Historical background

In the wake of the Reformation in Ireland, and with the later turbulent upheavals of the Cromwellian, Williamite and Penal eras of the seventeenth and eighteenth centuries, Catholic episcopal organisation suffered severe disruption, with bishops often being exiled from their dioceses. During intermittent phases of active persecution, bishops, far from hoarding records, needed to distance themselves from their own potentially incriminating papers. In 1713 for example, Edmund Byrne, archbishop of Dublin, was ordered by the lords justices and council to 'be apprehended and committed to jail and his papers to be sealed up and sent to the Council offices'. In addition to the losses induced by penal restriction, other factors leading to the wholesale or partial destruction of episcopal records included natural disasters, such as flood and fire, and the passing of those papers into family hands on the death of a prelate.

From about the middle of the eighteenth century, bishops began, tentatively at first, to keep records, a development interpreted by historians as indicating that Catholic episcopal organisation had by this time been firmly re-established, and that the efficacy of the penal laws was waning. As the Catholic revival in Ireland accelerated in the early decades of the nineteenth century, and bishops developed the pastoral infrastructure of their dioceses, promoted devotional reform and innovation, and negotiated with government, so their correspondence broadened and multiplied. The advent of a new cheap postal service and advances in educational provision added appreciably to the weight of episcopal post-bags. However, the accumulation and survival of episcopal collections in the nineteenth century was greatly hampered by the absence of a basic archival tradition which would allow for the automatic preservation, in diocesan hands, of the papers of successive bishops. Some bishops destroyed their papers as a matter of course to preserve confidentiality, to suppress diocesan quarrels and to shield their actions from their successors. 'I keep very few letters', Archbishop Thomas Croke of Cashel admitted in a letter to Michael Davitt in 1892. Four decades previously, Paul Cullen had arrived at Drogheda as the new archbishop of Armagh. 'Not a scrap of paper in the archives', he bitterly complained in a letter to a friend in Rome. 'Not even to tell me the names of the priests'. The fact that each bishop had to make his own arrangements with regard to accommodation further militated against the survival of episcopal archives.

The slowly developing archival consciousness in the Catholic Church in Ireland was greatly enhanced by the reforming Synod of Thurles in 1850. The Synod deplored the loss up to that time of so many documents and decreed means to be taken to 'obviate such an evil'. Bishops were required to 'erect and constitute in each of their respective dioceses an archive in the safest and most commodious place possible'. The Synod outlined specific classes of records which were to be preserved in diocesan archives as follows:

> All documents relating to the origins and history of the diocese; those referring to matrimonial dispensations and judgements; to provisions of benefices and unions and divisions of parishes; privileges and indulgences granted to the diocese itself or to the cathedral church or to a parish church; and those which bear in any way on the proper administration of the diocese.

The impetus for archival reform was strengthened by the promulgation of the Code of Canon Law in 1917. The Code, which set out norms for administrative and juridical procedure in the Church throughout the world, not only required each bishop to safeguard the record of the diocesan curia, but also charged him with the responsibility of ensuring that 'archive records and documents of cathedral, collegial, parochial and other churches on his territory be adequately conserved'. Whilst the Code and national and provincial synods held in Ireland provided an essential framework for Church archival policy, and for the preservation of archives, it would be unwise to assume that their strictures were followed automatically, or even in full measure. Bishops continued to burn their papers and the survival of archives was rendered the more problematic by the slow rate at which dioceses fixed on permanent episcopal residences during the period from 1850 to 1970. (The loss or survival of episcopal collections is more fully discussed in David C. Sheehy's 'Archives of the Catholic Church in Ireland' in Reamann Ó Muiri (ed.), *Irish Church history today* (Armagh, 1990)).

Archival holdings

For all of the difficulties encountered in developing an archival tradition in the Catholic Church in Ireland, what material has survived in diocesan archives down to the present time? We know that of the twenty-six dioceses, seven have records dating from the second half of the eighteenth century, ten from the nineteenth century, and the final nine from this century. Overall, half of the total only have material dating from about the middle of the last century. The uneven nature of record survival is indicated by the fact that some diocesan archives have significant gaps in their records post-dating the period when record keeping for most dioceses began to follow a reasonably consistent pattern. Thus the diocesan archives of Down and Connor manifest a lacuna in their episcopal collections for the period from 1866 to 1929 whilst those of Ardagh and Clonmacnoise hold very little material from 1895. If diocesan archives were to be rated in terms of the richness and importance of their holdings, the three archdioceses of Armagh, Cashel and Dublin would be set first, followed by Cork, Kerry, Kildare and Leighlin and Down and Connor. A particular feature of Irish diocesan archives is the way in which, in a small number of cases, collections migrate, as it were, from one diocese to another. This happened when a suffragan bishop was promoted to an archbishopric and took his papers with him to his new posting. In this regard, the diocesan archives of Raphoe and Clonfert, in particular, have suffered when, in the past, their bishops were translated to Armagh and Tuam respectively. In more recent times, this practice has ceased, due to the increasing complexity of modern diocesan administration, and in the case of Raphoe, the diocesan archivist has succeeded in having material relating to Raphoe transferred from Armagh to its original location.

The holdings of diocesan archives can be sub-divided into a number of records series: diocesan chapter records; episcopal papers; papers of priests and laity; and records of diocesan agencies and organisations. On occasion, the records of diocesan colleges and parish records may be found among the holdings of diocesan archives. Chapter records relate to the formal proceedings of a body, traditionally associated with a cathedral, which also acted as consultative council to the bishop in the diocese. Episcopal papers cover the records associated with an individual bishop's term of office. They are the largest and richest collections of archives to be found in a diocesan repository and they most consistently contain material of interest to local historians. They usually consist of private office papers, which include family papers and records of a bishop's priestly career, prior to his elevation to high office; general correspondence files covering everyday administration under such categories as the Holy See, government and hierarchy, priests, religious and laity; chancellery files relating to ordinations, dispensations and matters of Church law; financial and legal records; files relating to diocesan agencies, organisations and commissions; literary material; maps and plans; photographs and film; press cuttings; sacred relics and episcopal memorabilia.

Visitation returns, that is those reports made prior to a visit by the local bishop, provide formal accounts of the state of churches and religious practice in particular parishes and vicariously include information on social and economic conditions in these localities. From about the middle of the nineteenth century, these returns were made on printed forms with parish clergy being required to furnish information under a set number of headings. The information which can be gleaned from these returns may be complemented by more anecdotal reporting on parish events in correspondence between

5. Visitation return for the parish of Blanchardstown, 1830
(Dublin Diocesan Archives)

parish clergy and bishops. It is thus possible to build up, over time, a reasonable picture of the nature and development of a given parish, its clergy and its laity.

Thus, for example, the parish of Ballymore Eustace, in County Kildare, is represented by a range of documents in the episcopal collections in the Dublin diocesan archives for the eighteenth and nineteenth centuries. The earliest document relating to the parish is a visitation return made by John Troy, archbishop of Dublin, in 1791. Five years on, the Troy papers reveal a series of letters concerning a quarrel between the parish priest, Father Michael Devoy, and Captain Richard Doyle, a member of the local gentry. Doyle accused Father Devoy of espousing the principles of the French Revolution, but Devoy, by way of reply, was able to muster thirty-nine affidavits signed by named parishioners in his own defence. In the papers of Archbishop Daniel Murray, Troy's successor, the researcher will discover visitation returns for Ballymore Eustace for the years 1833, 1837 and 1840.

The returns show that the parish had a population of 4,000 adults in 1833. It had twelve schools, each attended by about forty children and two confraternities of St John the Evangelist which provided catechetical instruction, assisted the dying and recited the Office of the Dead. In addition, Ballymore Eustace possessed a parochial library of about 350 volumes. In 1868, the parish priest, Canon Frederick Bell, forwarded, at the request of the archbishop, Cardinal Paul Cullen, a report on the schools in his parish detailing the numbers in attendance, their management, and denominational influence over the students. Finally, in the papers of Archbishop Edward McCabe, there appears a letter from the then parish priest of Ballymore Eustace, Father Joseph Horgan, dated August 1879, reporting on the crime and disorder at Poulaphuca Waterfall which coincided each year with the Feast of the Assumption.

Aside from preserving episcopal collections, diocesan archives have provided an unexpected but felicitous refuge for other kinds of collections including the papers of priests and members of the laity, and the records of diocesan and secular organisations. Thus, for example, the Dublin diocesan archives holds the combined surviving records of the Catholic Association, the New Catholic Association and the Loyal National Repeal Association, organisations which, under the able leadership of Daniel O'Connell, flourished as vehicles for mass, non-violent, Catholic agitation in Ireland in the first half of the nineteenth century. The diocesan archives of Galway preserve the records of the wardenship for the period 1730 to 1831, a rich source for local historical research. Like many other diocesan archives Galway also has a series of files relating to each of the parishes of the diocese which have been built up over the course of the last two centuries and which are quite distinct from the main episcopal collections. Kilmore diocesan archives has the papers of a number of priest historians and antiquarians of the diocese, including those of the Rev. Philip O'Connell (1827–1903), Owen F. Traynor (1897–1988) and T.P. Cunningham (1922–1986). Killaloe's holdings include the notebooks of Canon John Clancy (1883–1964) and a series of parish history files based on questionnaire returns relating to antiquities, folklore and churches, compiled in the 1940s by Dermot F. Gleeson, author of *A History of the Diocese of Killaloe* (Dublin, 1962).

How to gain access to diocesan archives

The records of the Catholic Church in Ireland are private records to which members of the public have no automatic legal right of access. However, most dioceses try to accommodate bona fide researchers to the best of their ability. Permission to consult records in diocesan archives is granted by the local bishop under whose jurisdiction they lie. There is no fixed policy governing access to diocesan archives to which all members of the Irish Catholic hierarchy must subscribe: each bishop devises his own rules and restrictions. Factors which influence access policy include the amount of resources available to a bishop to allow him to provide a proper archives service; the richness and value of collections in the archives; their state of order or disorder; and the availability of a diocesan archivist to manage the archives and the requirements of researchers. Though bishops in general like to follow norms adhered to by their confrères, each of the twenty-six dioceses in Ireland has its own particular history and circumstances which shape policy with regard to access to their diocesan archives.

In such a varied landscape how is the local historian to discern which dioceses have kept good records and can accommodate researchers? Fortunately, there are a number of published works which offer essential orientation and a helpful starting point. Firstly, the researcher should consult the *Directory of Irish Archives*, edited by Seamus Helferty and Raymond Refaussé and published by the Irish Academic Press. The third edition of the *Directory* was published in 1999 and contains entries for diocesan archives in twenty-one of the twenty-six dioceses in Ireland. The entries provide concise and practical information such as postal and e-mail addresses, telephone and fax numbers, the point of contact, hours of opening and facilities (such as photocopying), published guides (if any), and a brief but useful résumé of major collections held by each repository.

In order to more precisely identify the point of contact for any given diocesan archives, researchers should turn to the *Irish Catholic Directory* which is published annually by Veritas. The *Directory* provides a detailed entry for each of the twenty-six dioceses, identifying the relevant bishop and diocesan archivist. In 1999 only half of the dioceses in Ireland could boast of having diocesan archivists. Moreover, of these, only a minority, such as those in Armagh, Cloyne and Dublin, were full-time appointees. The remainder were priest historians who, burdened with pastoral or academic responsibilities, and in spite of their best efforts, were in no position to provide a proper diocesan archives service. In recent years, the dioceses of Galway, Clonfert and Kilmore have employed consultant archivists to put their archives in good order and list the main collections but, as a general rule, if a diocese does not have a diocesan archivist, access to its archives is extremely problematic. Researchers are best advised, when seeking access to diocesan archives, to make first contact by letter with a diocesan archivist or the local bishop. This will allow researchers to properly introduce themselves, establish their bona fides, and set out clearly the nature and scope of their research topic.

Having consulted the above-named directories and identified a diocesan archives as a likely source of archival material relevant to their research, researchers should seek to determine if there is any published material relating to that particular repository. Accordingly, researchers should be aware of the fact that a number of useful reports on diocesan archives in Ireland have been published in periodicals over the past thirty years or so, as have calendars of some of the most important collections of archiepiscopal papers. In addition, researchers should note that a small and select number of collections are available for consultation on microfilm, subject to written permission from the relevant bishop, in the National Library of Ireland. Published reports on diocesan archives include Mark Tierney's 'Cashel diocesan archives' in *Proceedings of the Irish Catholic Historical Committee*, (1965–7) and his later report of the same title on the same repository in Mark Tierney (ed.), *Thurles: the cathedral town* (Thurles, 1989); Raymond Murray's 'The Armagh diocesan archives' in *Archivium Hibernicum*, xxxii (1974); Mary Purcell's 'Sidelights on the Dublin diocesan archives' in *Archivium Hibernicum*, xxxvi (1981) and David Sheehy's 'The archives of the archdiocese of Dublin' in *Catholic Archives*, ix (1989); Angela Bolster's 'The archives of the diocese of Cork and Ross' in *Catholic Archives*, viii (1988); Jan Power's 'Galway diocesan archives' in *Archivium Hibernicum*, xlvi (1991–92); Linus Walker's 'Diocesan archives of Kildare and Leighlin' in *Newsletter*, the organ of the Association of Church Archivists of Ireland, xvii (1997) and Edward Daly's 'Derry diocesan archives' in the same publication, xviii (1998). Calendars of the papers of a select number of bishops from the eighteenth and nineteenth centuries have been published. Mark Tierney has provided calendars of the papers of successive archbishops of Cashel in *Collectanea Hibernica* as follows: James Butler II, 1773–91 in vols xviii and xix (1977) and xx (1978); Michael Slattery, 1822–48, in vols xxx (1988), xxxi and xxxii (1989–90), xxxiii (1991), xxxiv and xxxv (1992–93), xxxvi and xxxvii (1994–95), and William Croke, 1841–1902 in vols xiii (1970), xvi (1973), xvii (1974–75). Calendars of the papers of Daniel Murray, archbishop of Dublin, from 1823 to 1852, prepared by Mary Purcell, have been published in *Archivium Hibernicum*, xxxvi–xli (1981–87) with an index provided in vol xli (1987). *Archivium* is currently publishing calendars of the papers of Murray's secretary, archdeacon John Hamilton, vols xliii– (1988–). A summary of the catalogue of the contents of Clogher diocesan archives, for the period 1788–1834, has been presented by John Forsythe in *Archivium Hibernicum*, xliii (1988). Copies of Clogher episcopal papers postdating 1834 are available for consultation on microfilm in the Public Record Office of Northern Ireland. The Record Office in Belfast also holds microfilm copies of the papers of successive archbishops of Armagh from 1819 to 1887.

II. COLLEGES AND SEMINARIES

Historical background

Colleges and seminaries are probably the most overlooked Catholic repositories in Ireland by local historians, and this in spite of the fact that many of them are of long standing and can boast of distinguished historians and antiquarians among their staff. Of the dozen or so institutions which fall into the 'seminaries and colleges' category, some are diocesan seminaries, some are secondary school academies (which in the past may have doubled as diocesan seminaries), whilst a third portion consist of teacher training establishments.

Half Yearly General Meeting held in Library on Sunday 22nd June 1873

Present Mr Bermingham M.P. in the Chair

Messrs T. Strahan E. Davis. C. Clancy John Keogh, N. Farmer, P. McKenna Jas Deegan E. Farmer Jas Redmond H. Lord E. Hamilton J. Cahill J. Clarke J. Regan N. McLaughlin John Deegan P. Maher

The minutes of the past quarter been read and after a few remarks were made as regards same. The president moved and Mr Jas Redmond seconded that the minutes as read be adopted. (Passed)

It was moved by Mr John Keogh and seconded by Mr R Connolly that the anniversary office for the repose of the soul of the late Daniel O'Connell be recited as usual in this Church and that the various Confraternities be summoned to attend. The office to be recited on the 3rd Tuesday of July 1873.

As an amendment Mr Strahan moved and Mr Hamilton seconded that instead of a public office that we recite the office in the church by the members of this confraternity only.

The amendment been put the votes went as follows 8 for and 10 against for the motion 10 for and 8 against the amendment was then declared lost.

The Election for president acting presidents and Council was then gone thro' and resulted in favour of the following

For Head President
  Mr John Bermingham   14 votes
  Edwd Hamilton   2 "

Mr Bermingham was declared reelected

6. Extract from the Confraternity Minute Book, parish of SS. Michael and John, Dublin, 1873 (Dublin Diocesan Archives)

The oldest of these colleges is St Kieran's in Kilkenny, which was founded in 1782, whilst the best known is St Patrick's, Maynooth, founded in 1795. During the seventeenth and eighteenth centuries Catholic student priests went to Irish colleges on the Continent for their training. Many of these colleges closed during the French Revolution and the opening of a national seminary at Maynooth foreshadowed the establishment of a small network of diocesan seminaries to provide seminary training at home in Ireland. This development was highlighted by the *Eighth Report of the Commission of Irish Education Inquiry*, which recorded in 1827 that there were 371 clerical students at Maynooth, 100 more in other Irish seminaries in Carlow, Kilkenny, Tuam, Waterford and Wexford, and a further 140 on the Continent.

Archival holdings

Over the past century and a half, these colleges have, with varying degrees of success, preserved their academic and administrative records. Whilst a college's own records, particularly student records, are of obvious genealogical interest, they can also, as in the case of Patrick's College, Maynooth, as Patrick J. Corish has noted, be 'an almost disappointingly routine and uneventful chronicle of a seminary' (Patrick J. Corish, 'Maynooth College archives' in *Catholic Archives*, xiii (1993)). Nevertheless, many of these colleges have become places of deposit for valuable collections of local historical archives which might not otherwise have been preserved. These collections have been gathered in by staff members with a strong passion for local history and antiquarianism, and blessed with a keen appreciation of the transient and fragile nature of archival documents.

St Patrick's College, Maynooth, as previously noted, is home to the Salamanca papers, but it also holds the historical papers collected by Laurence Renehan, president of the college (1845–57) and noted collector of Irish historical manuscripts, and the papers of John Francis Shearman (1830–85), the Kilkenny born antiquary and genealogist. The latter include pedigrees of Kilkenny families and drawings and antiquarian notes on Kilkenny, Dunlavin and Howth. St Kieran's in Kilkenny houses the manuscripts of Canon William Carrigan (1860–1924). These consist of 167 notebooks compiled by Carrigan in the 1880s in preparation for his monumental *History and Antiquities of the Diocese of Ossory* (Dublin, 1905). These notebooks, among other things, contain priceless testamentary abstracts from documents lost in the destruction of the Public Record Office of Ireland in 1922. The college also holds the collections of the Rev Edward Dowling (1886–1960), Philip Moore (1812–1888), William Healy (1842–1923), James Graves (1816–1886) and T.J. Clohosey (1906–1969). Moore, Graves and Healy were founder members of the Kilkenny Archaeological Society forerunner of the Royal Society of Antiquaries of Ireland. Similarly, St Patrick's College, Thurles, opened in 1837, preserves important local historical material collated by distinguished members of its staff. Its four outstanding collections are those of the Rev William Maher (1872–1937), Walter Skehan (1905–1971), Phil Fogarty (1889–1976) and Richard Devane (1890–1959). The first collection belongs to the College and the latter three are held on behalf of Cashel diocesan archives. Maher was the first significant chronicler of his native archdiocese and his work was drawn on by his successors. The four collections consist of manuscript notes, gathered from a wide variety of sources, on the ecclesiastical and civil history of the archdiocese of Cashel and Emly and of County Tipperary. The Maher Papers include a diary kept by Father Maher during the War of Independence and the formative years of the Irish State. The College's archives also possess diaries kept by the Revv. Thomas and James O'Carroll during the mid-nineteenth century which have been privately published by Father James Feehan, parish priest of Boherlahan in County Tipperary. The Skehan Papers include a complete biographical index of the clergy of the archdiocese of Cashel and the Hayes Papers contain a comprehensive dossier on every known ecclesiastical site in the diocese. Finally, the College archives preserves a register of the parish of Boherlahan, for the period 1736–40. St Peter's College, in Wexford, has the Hore manuscripts, which shed much light on the history of Wexford. St Peter's also holds valuable local history collections compiled by the Revv. Thaddeus O'Byrne, Christopher Flood and Robert Ranson.

Gaining access to college and seminary archives

College archives suffer from the same deficiencies as diocesan archives such as low levels of financial provision, a paucity of full-time trained archivists, poor or even non-existent finding aids, a lack of published guides and inadequate facilities for visiting researchers. The researcher should adopt similar strategies to gaining access to these records as they would do in the case of other Church archives. Researchers should consult the *Irish Catholic Directory* and the *Directory of Irish Archives* to identify archival office holders and the range of records and facilities offered by individual repositories. Researchers will find that, invariably, the designated college archivist is a full-time member of the college teaching staff, with many calls on his or her time. This should be taken into account when first making contact. Arriving without prior notification is likely to prove as frustrating an exercise for the unannounced caller as it will prove irritating for the archivist. A prior appointment would be essential to gain access to these archives and the dispatch of a polite, explanatory letter is the more likely to elicit a courteous and co-operative response.

With the exception of Patrick J. Corish's report on the Maynooth College archives (see above), researchers will find it difficult to locate published reports on the archival collections of Catholic colleges and seminaries in Ireland. However, useful information can be gleaned from official histories such as

Holy Cross College, Clonliffe, Dublin 1859–1959 (Dublin, 1959), and Fearghus O Fearghail's *St Kieran's College, Kilkenny, 1782–1982* (Kilkenny, 1982). John McEvoy's *Carlow College, 1793–1993* (Carlow, 1993), is particularly useful as it contains short biographical entries for all ordained priests and members of the teaching staff. Much less detail is given in Patrick J. Hamill's *Maynooth students and ordinations index, 1795–1895* (Maynooth, 1982) and his *Maynooth students and ordinations, 1895–1984* (Maynooth, 1984).

Researchers should be aware that it is possible to gain access to some college records at a remove. The account books of St Patrick's College, Carlow, the main source of information on early students of the college from 1793, are available on microfilm in the National Library of Ireland. The latter repository also holds a microfilm of the Carrigan notebooks from Kilkenny. An index to Carrigan's abstracts from 952 wills was published in *The Irish Genealogist* in 1970. A project to index the archives of St Patrick's College, Thurles, is currently underway, and when completed it is planned to make the results available to researchers through Tipperary County Library.

III. PARISH RECORDS

Historical background

The best known records of the Catholic Church in Ireland are those created at parish level. Parish clergy have been obliged to keep formal records of sacramental occasions since the Council of Trent (1545–63). From the seventeenth century, Catholic synods of bishops in Ireland exhorted parish clergy to maintain registers of baptisms and marriages. However, sporadic persecution and consequent disruption to ecclesiastical organisation meant that only in a handful of cases, such as in the town of Wexford, were these instructions carried out. Thus it was not until the relaxation of the penal laws in the latter part of the eighteenth century that priests began to maintain such records in significant numbers.

Kevin Whelan, in a pioneering essay ('The Regional Impact of Irish Catholicism 1700–1850', in W.J. Smyth and Kevin Whelan (ed.), *Common Ground: essays on the historical geography of Ireland*, Cork, 1988) delineated the regional variations in the Catholic revival in Ireland by mapping parishes throughout the island on the basis of the oldest surviving parish registers. He found that the overwhelming majority of these registers dated from the nineteenth century with the bulk of these belonging to the period 1800 to 1845, when the Catholic renaissance was well under way. Whelan also found that a significant number dated from the last quarter of the eighteenth century. These were generated in towns and ports linked to their settled and prosperous hinterlands with an identifiable Catholic heartland located south and east of a line running roughly from Dundalk to Athlone to Limerick to Dingle. By contrast, a significant number of first-surviving registers in the Ulster/Connacht region post-dated 1870. In the archdiocese of Dublin, the oldest surviving registers are to be found in the city parishes of St Catherine, Meath Street, dating from 1740, St Andrew, Westland Row, dating from 1742, and St Nicholas, Francis Street, also dating from 1742. In the rural parts of the archdiocese, the oldest registers are those held by Athy parish, dating back to 1743, Wicklow town parish, dating from 1747, while other country parishes can boast of survivals from the 1780s.

Registers of baptisms, marriages and burials

Unlike Church of Ireland registers which record details of baptisms, marriages and burials Catholic parish registers generally consist only of records of baptisms and marriages. Only a small number of parishes have maintained death or burial records dating back to the nineteenth century and even then the registers only run for a limited or inconsistent number of years. Out of 1,042 parishes whose registers have been microfilmed by the National Library of Ireland, only 214 have been found to have kept burial records.

The early register books, which were in use in the seventeenth and eighteenth centuries, have survived in different shapes and sizes. It was not until the middle of the nineteenth century that volumes of a standardised size and format, with printed headings and column divisions, were increasingly adopted. Entries are made in chronological order and in manuscript. Some of the handwriting will pose a considerable challenge to the reader. English or Latin was used and sometimes a combination of both. Places and surnames are given in English only but Christian names have sometimes been rendered in Latin. A greater difficulty is posed by the use of Latin terms to describe relationships and status. There are, however, only a set number of such terms used and lists of these and their English equivalents can be found in James Ryan (ed.), *Irish Church records* (Dublin, 1992) and in Maire MacConghaill and Paul Gorry's *Tracing Irish ancestors* (Glasgow, 1997). The significance of Catholic parish registers of baptisms, marriages and burials, in research terms, as noted by Ryan, is that they are often

> the only evidence of the existence of a large proportion of the population of Ireland in the eighteenth and nineteenth centuries, especially those who did not own or formally lease land; nor make wills or deeds; nor join armies or societies; nor sign petitions; nor live in areas for which census information survives.

Parish registers can also prove to be unexpected records for information relating to important historical events in the life of a parish. For example,

Edward MacLysaght reported in *Analecta Hibernica*, xv (1944) that the register of baptisms and marriages in the parish of Clonrush, County Clare, also contained the minutes of a local relief committee operating during the Great Famine in 1846.

How to gain access to parish records

Parish records, as with all other records of the Catholic Church in Ireland, are private records to which the public have no automatic legal right of access. Parish records are the property of the Church as a whole but as with all aspects of parochial administration they come under the purview of the local bishop. Thus, while the parish priest is the custodian of the records it is the bishop of the diocese who dictates policy with regard to access to parish archives. The general approach adopted by bishops in relation to access to parish records is the same as that governing their approach to the question of access to diocesan archives. On the one hand, they wish to accommodate, in so far as is reasonable and practical, bona fide researchers. On the other hand, they are concerned to preserve confidentiality, where that is appropriate, and to defend their rights as holders of the copyright of these records.

a. Original registers

As original registers are, in almost all cases, kept in the custody of their creating parish, it might be assumed that this is where they can be most easily accessed. However, this is not necessarily the case. Though parish priests do allow researchers to use original registers, it is usually easier to gain access to these records in copy format or through a computerised index in libraries, archival repositories and heritage centres. Parish clergy will expect researchers who approach them seeking access to originals to have exhausted every opportunity to gain access to their records through other means. In any case, before seeking access to parish records, in whatever format, researchers should attempt to establish if the relevant material is extant. Recourse may be had to the list of microfilmed parish registers held by the National Library of Ireland. In addition, an incomplete but still useful list of Catholic parish registers, known to have survived down to the early part of the twentieth century, will be found in *Archivium Hibernicum*, iii (1914).

b. Microfilm copies

In the 1950s and 1960s, the Catholic Church in Ireland co-operated with a project undertaken by the National Library of Ireland to preserve on microfilm all of the earliest surviving parish registers of baptisms and marriages. As already noted, the commencement dates for the oldest registers varied from the eighteenth century for counties on the eastern and southern seaboard to the mid-nineteenth century for counties on the western seaboard. The year 1888 was chosen as the cut-off date for the microfilming of registers as, by that date, the civil registration of births and marriages was well under way (the Civil Registration Act came into force in 1864).

As a result of this initiative, the National Library today holds microfilm copies of the earliest registers of most Catholic parishes in Ireland (including parishes in Northern Ireland). Researchers should note, however, that for various reasons, not all parish registers were copied and that some of those that were had been in a poor state of preservation. Microfilms of registers from parishes in most Catholic dioceses are freely available for consultation in the National Library in Dublin. However, researchers seeking to gain access to microfilms of registers from the dioceses of Cashel, Kerry and Limerick, must first obtain a letter of authorisation from the appropriate bishop. In most instances such permission is granted by return of post, fax or e-mail. (See appendix 1: list of the Catholic dioceses of Ireland and permanent addresses of bishops). The microfilms for the registers of the diocese of Limerick are also available in the Mid-West regional archives in Limerick. Those intending to consult microfilms at the National Library should read the Library's *Family research leaflet number 2: Parish registers in the National Library of Ireland* and its *List of parish registers on microfilm*, both of which are available in the main reading room in Kildare Street.

c. Heritage centres

A decade ago, the Irish Genealogical Project, a Government-sponsored initiative, was launched to provide a network of heritage centres offering services to genealogical researchers on a countrywide basis. In the intervening period, the government has withdrawn as the main sponsor of this enterprise which is now co-ordinated by a private company, Irish Genealogy Limited. Nevertheless, more than thirty heritage centres have embarked upon a programme of building up computerised databases of records of essential value to genealogical researchers. Much of this work has centred on indexing Catholic parish registers, with the co-operation of the relevant diocesan authorities. However, not all dioceses have agreed to co-operate with such indexing projects because of difficulties relating to copyright and confidentiality. Researchers should be aware that the heritage centres do not offer direct access to their databases but rather offer a fee-based research service to their customers.

IV. THE ARCHIVES OF RELIGIOUS ORDERS

Historical background

For most researchers, the archives of Irish religious orders, congregations and societies represent uncharted territory. However, they are a potentially exciting new source for a variety of research fields – not least that of local history. Religious orders have made an enormous contribution to the history of the Catholic Church in Ireland and to the country as a whole. Long-standing orders such as the Cistercians represent a link with the golden age of Irish monasticism, which underpinned the survival of European civilisation after the fall of the Roman Empire and created a unique manuscript heritage to which all Christian denominations in Ireland today are heirs.

The Franciscans, Dominicans and Jesuits were to the fore during the Counter-Reformation in Ireland (c.1560–1630) and later. As the Catholic revival unfolded its most remarkable feature was the dramatic expansion of Catholic religious communities in the nineteenth century, a development whose momentum carried it forward well into the twentieth century. The growth of female religious communities in Ireland was undoubtedly the most remarkable phenomenon. In 1800 there were in Ireland a mere 120 nuns, based in eleven houses, belonging to six religious orders. By 1900 there were over 8,000 women religious, in 327 convents, belonging to thirty-seven religious orders. Irish foundations such as the Presentation Order, the Mercy Order, the Irish Sisters of Charity, the Sisters of the Holy Faith, and male religious orders such as the Christian Brothers and the Presentation Brothers were at the forefront of this prodigious expansion of religious life. The phenomenal growth in vocational enrolment translated into an equally prodigious output reflected in the provision of educational, welfare and health services, and also resulted in the creation of a large mass of record material.

From the 1970s onwards, a marked fall-off in vocations began to impact on Irish religious communities, necessitating an orderly restructuring. By the middle of the following decade, convents, monasteries and homes began to close as orders consolidated and reordered their priorities according to available personnel resources. The closure served to focus attention on long forgotten but still accumulating archives and came at a time when religious orders were just beginning to face up to their archival responsibilities.

Archival holdings

As with other record-creating agencies within the Catholic Church in Ireland, the archives of religious have enjoyed mixed fortunes. While some congregations and societies have been scrupulous about record keeping and preservation, for many others archival consciousness has only dawned in relatively recent times. Among the factors which have mitigated against the survival of religious archives the following have been identified by Marianne Cosgrave in *Irish Archives*, iv, no. 2 (1997): 'the natural attrition that occurs over a long period; the absence of a coherent record creation and management system; accidental loss; over-zealous housekeeping; or deliberate destruction to save space or protect sensitivities.'

Records kept by religious include annals, documents relating to the foundation of a congregation or society, institutional records of schools, orphanages and homes administered by religious, financial records, personnel records and correspondence files. The annals provide a day to day record of the internal workings of a religious community and, of particular interest to local historians, they also record the degree to which external events impact on that community. For example, the annals of the Redemptoristine monastery at Clonliffe, in Dublin record the response of the community to a passing procession in July 1862 to a field nearby where the foundation stone was laid for a proposed campus for the Catholic University of Ireland:

> No Benediction on account of the laying of the first stone for the Catholic University in one of the fields near our garden. We had to stop the recital aloud of Vespers, for at the very time, the procession of carriages and bands playing the national airs was passing our windows to the ceremony; the noise was too great for us to hear one another. The trees were decorated with flags. Twenty-four archbishops and bishops were present but Dr Cullen was prevented by illness from attending. When Vespers were concluded we went into the garden and Reverend Mother kindly allowed us to listen to the music – we amused ourselves much.

The records of institutions run by religious permit a glimpse into the lives of the poor and the marginalised who might not otherwise be represented in archival records. Personnel records include registers of entrants or professions which record the entrant's name, address, name of parents, date of birth, date of entrance, date of profession and date of death. Additional personnel records would include wills, certificates of birth and death, diaries, testimonials, obituaries and, in the case of female religious, dowry records. Dowries were presented by entrants from well-off backgrounds, who were known as choir sisters. Recruits from poor backgrounds, who were called lay-sisters, did not offer dowries. Thus all strands of Irish society can be said to be represented in the archives of Irish female religious orders.

Among male religious orders in Ireland a number stand out as having important holdings of archival material of relevance to the study of Irish local history. The doyen of male religious repositories is surely the library of the Franciscan House of Studies. Located at Killiney, County Dublin since 1945, the Franciscan library combines notable collections relating to Franciscan house in Ireland and abroad, precious Gaelic manuscripts and a wide range of other manuscripts relating to modern Irish history. The provincial archives of the Irish Dominicans, at Tallaght, contains collections relating to Dominican houses in Ireland and Portugal. The international character of Irish religious holdings is again reflected in the collections of the Irish Jesuit archives; yet this repository is also home to an extraordinary range of collections of papers of notable churchmen and laymen from the nineteenth and twentieth centuries. Finally, mention must be made of the Cistercian Abbey at Mount Melleray whose archives include the invaluable historical papers of Canon William Burke.

How to gain access to religious archives

The decline in the fortunes of religious orders in Ireland has coincided with a new found appreciation by religious of their archival inheritance. Religious orders have, in recent times, not only displayed a concern for preservation of their records but also a cautious willingness to open them up to the scrutiny of outside researchers. Over the past two decades religious archives have been the single greatest area of growth in the archival sphere in Ireland. This development was reflected in the fact that religious archives accounted for forty of the 249 entries in the third edition of the *Directory of Irish Archives* (Dublin, 1999). However, the fact that a significant proportion of the religious archives listed in the *Directory* could not, at that time, accommodate personal visits by researchers, indicated that many religious archives in Ireland were still only in the preliminary stages of reorganisation. The uneven rate of progress made to-date by congregations and societies in coming to grips with their records inevitably means that researchers will enjoy varying degrees of success when seeking access to religious archives. Researchers seeking access to the archives of religious congregations and societies that have entries in the *Directory of Irish Archives* are advised to apply, in writing, to the archivist or the relevant religious order. In the case of congregations and societies that are not listed in the *Directory of Irish Archives*, researchers should apply, in writing, to the head, whose name and address will be found in the *Irish Catholic Directory*.

Published guides and reports relating to Irish religious archives, though few in number, are a useful starting point. Those delving into female religious archives are well served by Marianne Cosgrave's 'An introduction to the archives of the Catholic congregations of women religious in Ireland, with particular reference to genealogical research' in *Irish Archives*, iv, no. 2 (1997). In 1874 the noted archivist, Sir John Gilbert, reported on religious manuscripts repatriated from St Isidore's in Rome to the Franciscan friary at Merchants' Quay, Dublin, for the Royal Commission on Historical Manuscripts. A later introduction to the expanding archival treasure trove at Killiney was provided by Canice Mooney's 'Franciscan Library, Killiney: a short guide' in *Archivium Hibernicum*, xviii (1955). To mark the library's golden jubilee, Benignus Millett and Anthony Lynch published *Dún Mhuire, Killiney, 1945–95: léann agus seanchas*, a most useful volume of history, bibliography and calendars. Other reports on individual orders include Tom Davitt's 'The archives of the Irish province of the congregation of the Missions (Franciscans)' published in

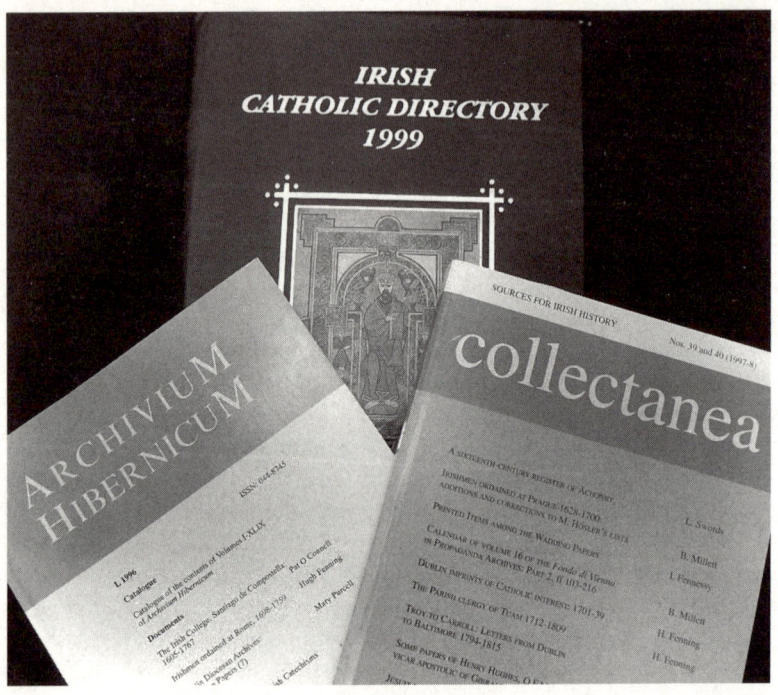

7. Essential works for researchers to consult: Irish Catholic Directory, Archivium Hibernicum, and Collectanea Hibernica

Catholic Archives, v (1985) and Magdalena Frisby's 'The archives and papers of the Sisters of Mercy at Carysfort Park' which also appeared in *Catholic Archives*, v (1985); Cora Richardson's 'The archives of the Missionary Sisters of the Holy Rosary' in *Catholic Archives*, xi (1991); Dominique Horgan's 'In our keeping: the archives of the congregation of the Dominican Sisters, Cabra' in *Catholic Archives*, xiv (1994); Stephen Redmond's 'A guide to the Irish Jesuit province archives' in *Archivium Hibernicum*, l (1996) updating Fergus O'Donoghue's 'Irish Jesuit archives' also in *Archivium Hibernicum*, xli (1986); Mary Bernadette O'Leary's 'The archives of the Sisters of Charity' in *Catholic Archives*, xvii (1997); Desmond J. Brown's summary description of the collections in the archives of St Mary's province of the Irish Christian Brothers in the *Newsletter* of the Association of Church Archivists of Ireland, xvii (1997) is supplemented by Noelle Dowling's 'Allen Library' in the same *Newsletter*, xix (1998).

DAVID C. SHEEHY

Conclusion

It may be helpful to say a few words on what contribution the local historian may hope to make to the general historical understanding of the Irish Catholic Church. As might indeed be expected, developments in Church history have tended to follow those in history generally. A little over a generation ago 'history' in effect meant political history. Church history mirrored this in that its primary concern could be summed up in the phrase 'Church and State'. Then, however, historians began to strike out in new directions, first, probably, to 'economic history' and then to 'social history'. Whatever the labels attached, there was no mistaking the trend – interest had very definitely shifted from the leaders in society to those lower down the scale, to the 'ordinary people' that students love to talk about, in spite of warnings of how hard it is to find things to say about them. While historians are beginning to stress again the importance of 'political' history, the developments in the many fields of social history have left an indelible mark.

The background to this shift in historians' interest is beyond question the great social and political changes of the twentieth century. Church history followed the same pattern for similar reasons. In Church as well as in State previously accepted structures had to face new questionings. Religion had to be set in a new framework best symbolised by the Second Vatican Council's message that Christianity was a way of life as well as a set of rules and structures. This in turn sparked historians' interest in what was often referred to as 'the pastoral mission'. A sense of new achievement may have concealed for a time the reflection that this new approach was in the context of what the clergy thought they were doing for the laity, and might be concealing the fact that what the laity really believed might in some respects be different from what the clergy were teaching them to believe. The final refinement may lie in the realisation that too clear a contrast must not be drawn between a 'book religion' of the clergy and a 'traditional religion' of the laity. All clergy started life as laity in a lay environment, and the influence can be persistent.

So, in the religious field, as indeed elsewhere, 'What is really going on?' is a suitable question. It is also a very local question. In Ireland as elsewhere, and perhaps even more than elsewhere, people's lives were bounded by quite small localities until the standardisation of life took place because of the development of modern communications. 'Traditional Irish Catholicism', in a phrase at least once much used, will not be really understood except by meticulous examination at the grassroots.

One final word. The 'grassroots' examination of the local Christianities has to be set in a broader vision of Christianity. A good general historical survey is indispensable. Among recent works it is hard to better *Christianity: the first two thousand years* (London, 1997). The author, David L. Edwards, is a distinguished Anglican cleric-scholar. He is genuinely ecumenical, in that he aims at a respectful understanding of all Christian communities; his learning is encyclopedic; and his style runs easily. A good encyclopedia is another indispensable tool, and here the most useful is the *New Catholic Encyclopedia* (15 vols, New York, 1967), with supplementary volumes xvi (1974) and xvii (1979).

On Irish Church history the following may be recommended: Patrick J. Corish (ed.), *A History of Irish Catholicism* (16 fascicules, Dublin, 1967–72, uncompleted); Patrick J. Corish, *The Irish Catholic experience* (Dublin, 1985); John Watt, *The Church in medieval Ireland* (Dublin, 1972); Colm Lennon, *Sixteenth Century Ireland: the Incomplete Conquest* (Dublin, 1994); Patrick J. Corish, *The Catholic Community in the Seventeenth and Eighteenth Centuries* (Dublin, 1981). For the nineteenth century an important starting point is Emmet Larkin's *History of the Roman Catholic Church in Ireland in the Nineteenth Century* (Chapel Hill, London and Dublin, 1975-96) whose seven volumes to date cover the period 1850 to 1891. Two important short studies of Irish Catholics in Europe have been mentioned in the text: John Silke, 'The Irish abroad in the age of the Counter-reformation' in T.W. Moody, F.X. Martin, F.J. Byrne (ed.), *A New History of Ireland*, iii (Oxford, 1976), pp 587–633; and for the eighteenth century Cathaldus Giblin, OFM, 'Irish Exiles in Catholic Europe' in Patrick J. Corish (ed.), *A History of Irish Catholicism*, iv, no. 3 (Dublin, 1971). For a list of Catholic diocesan histories see appendix 2.

Appendix 1:
List of Catholic dioceses of Ireland and permanent addresses of bishops

Province of Armagh:

Archbishop of Armagh:	Ara Coeli, Armagh BT61 7QY Email admin@aracoeli.com
Bishop of Ardagh & Clonmacnois:	St Michael's, Longford Email ardaghi@iol.ie
Bishop of Clogher:	Bishop's House, Monaghan
Bishop of Derry:	Bishop's House, St Eugene's Cathedral, Derry BT49 9AP Email derrydiocese@aol.com
Bishop of Down & Connor:	Lisbreen, 73 Somerton Road, Belfast BT15 4DE
Bishop of Dromore:	Bishop's House, 44 Armagh Road, Newry, Co. Down BT35 6PN Email bishopofdromore@btinternet.com
Bishop of Kilmore:	Bishop's House, Cullies, Co Cavan Email kilmdioc@eircom.net
Bishop of Meath:	Bishop's House, Dublin Road, Mullingar, Co Westmeath Email bishmeath@eircom.net
Bishop of Raphoe:	Ard Adhamhnain, Letterkenny, Co Donegal Email raphoe@indigo.ie

Province of Dublin

Archbishop of Dublin: Archbishop's House, Drumcondra, Dublin 9

Bishop of Kildare & Leighlin: Bishop's House, Carlow
Email bishopkandl@eircom.net

Bishop of Ferns: Bishop's House, Summerhill, Wexford
Email brencom@ferns.ie

Bishop of Ossory: Sion House, Kilkenny

Province of Cashel

Archbishop of Cashel: Archbishop's House, Thurles,
Co Tipperary
Email cashelemly@eircom.net

Bishop of Cloyne: Cloyne Diocesan Centre, Cobh, Co Cork
Email cloyne@indigo.ie

Bishop of Cork & Ross: Cork & Ross Diocesan Offices,
Redemption Road, Cork

Bishop of Kerry: Bishop's House, Killarney, Co Kerry
Email bishopshouse@eircom.net

Bishop of Killaloe: Westbourne, Ennis, Co Clare

Bishop of Limerick: Limerick Diocesan Office,
66 O'Connell Street, Limerick
Email diocoff@eircom.net

Bishop of Waterford & Lismore: Bishop's House, John's Hill, Waterford

Province of Tuam

Archbishop of Tuam: Archbishop's House, Tuam, Co Galway

Appendix 1

Bishop of Achonry:	Bishop's House, Ballaghaderreen,
	Co Roscommon
	Email stnathys@eircom.net

Bishop of Clonfert:	St. Brendan's, Coorheen, Loughrea,
	Co Galway
	Email bpkirby@iol.ie

Bishop of Elphin:	St. Mary's, Sligo

Bishop of Killala:	Bishop's House, Ballina, Co Mayo
	Email deocilala@eircom.net

Bishop of Galway,	Mount St. Mary's, Taylor's Hill, Galway
Kilmacduagh & Kilfenora:

Addresses of seminaries and colleges

Pontifical Irish College, Rome	Via dei SS Quatro 1, Roma 00184
	E-mail ufficio@irishcollege.org

Irish College, Paris	5 Rue des Irlandais, 75005 Paris

St Patrick's College	Maynooth, Co Kildare
	Email presoff@may.ie

Holy Cross College	Clonliffe, Dublin 3

St John's College	John's Hill, Waterford

St Kieran's College	Kilkenny
	Email skc1782@iol.ie

St Patrick's College	Carlow
	Email stafspcc@rtc-carlow.ie

St Patrick's College	Thurles, Co Tipperary
	Email luceat@eircom.net

St Peter's College	Wexford

Appendix 2:
Handlist of Catholic diocesan histories

ACHONRY	Swords, Liam	*A Hidden Church. The Diocese of Achonry 1689–1818* (Dublin, 1997).
ARDAGH & CLONMACNOIS	Kelly, James	'The Catholic Church in the Diocese of Ardagh', in Raymond Gillespie and Gerard Moran (eds), *Longford: Essays in County History* (Dublin, 1991).
	McNamee, James Joseph	*History of the Diocese of Ardagh* (Dublin, 1954).
	Monaghan, John	*Records relating to the Diocese of Ardagh & Clonmacnoise* (Dublin, 1886).
ARMAGH	Gwynn, Aubrey	*The medieval province of Armagh, 1470–1545* (Dundalk, 1946).
	Stewart, James	*Historical Memoirs of the City of Armagh* (revised by Ambrose Coleman O.P., Dublin, 1900).
CASHEL & EMLY	Maher, Michael	*The archbishops of Cashel* (Dublin, 1927).
CORK & ROSS	Bolster, Evelyn	*A history of the Diocese of Cork c.600–1886* (4 vols, Cork, 1972–93).
	Holland, William	*History of West Cork and the Diocese of Ross* (Skibbereen, 1950).
DERRY	Jefferies, Henry A. & Kieran Devlin (eds)	*History of the Diocese of Derry* (Dublin, 1999).

Appendix 2

DOWN & CONNOR	O'Laverty, James	*An historical account of the Diocese of Down and Connor, ancient and modern* (5 vols, Dublin, 1878–95. Reissued by Davidson Books, Belfast, 1980–82).
DUBLIN	D'Alton, John	*The Memoirs of the Archbishops of Dublin* (Dublin, 1838).
	Donnelly, Nicholas	*A short history of some Dublin parishes* (17 parts, Dublin, 1904–17. Reissued by Carraig Books in the 1970's).
	Kelly, James & Keogh, Daire (eds)	*History of the Catholic Diocese of Dublin* (Dublin, 1999).
	Moran, Patrick F.	*History of the Catholic Archbishops of Dublin since the Reformation* (Dublin, 1864).
ELPHIN	Burke, Francis	*Loch Ce and its annals, North Roscommon and the diocese of Elphin in times of old* (Dublin, 1895).
FERNS	Flood, William H. Grattan	*History of the diocese of Ferns* (Waterford, 1916).
GALWAY, KILMACDUAGH & KILFENORA	Fahey, Jerome	*The History and Antiquities of the Diocese of Kilmacduagh* (Dublin, 1893).
	Coen, Martin	*The Wardenship of Galway* (Galway, 1984).
KILDARE & LEIGHLIN	Brenan, Martin	*Schools of Kildare & Leighlin 1775–1835* (Dublin, 1935).
	Comerford, Michael	*Collections relating to the Dioceses of Kildare & Leighlin* (3 vols, Dublin, [1883–86]).

KILLALOE	Dwyer, Canon	*The diocese of Killaloe, from the Reformation to the close of the 18th century* (Dublin, 1878).
	Gwynn, Aubrey & Gleeson, Dermot F.	*A History of the Diocese of Killaloe Vol 1* (Dublin, 1962)
	Murphy Ignatius	*History of the Diocese of Killaloe 1700 to 1904* (3 vols, Dublin 1991–95).
KILMORE	O'Connell, Philip	*The Diocese of Kilmore, its history and antiquities* (Dublin, 1937).
	MacKiernan, Francis J.	*Diocese of Kilmore, Bishops and Priests 1136–1988* (Cavan, 1989).
	Gallogly, Daniel	*The Diocese of Kilmore 1800–1950* (Dublin, 1999).
LIMERICK	Begley, John	*The Diocese of Limerick, ancient and medieval* (Dublin, 1906).
	Begley, John	*The Diocese of Limerick in the 16th and 17th centuries* (Dublin, 1927).
	Begley, John	*The Diocese of Limerick from 1691 to the present time* (Dublin, 1938).
MEATH	Brady, John	*A short history of the parishes of the Diocese of Meath 1867–1937* (Navan, 1937).
	Cogan, Anthony	*The Ecclesiastical History of the Diocese of Meath, Ancient and Modern* (3 vols, Dublin, 1867–74. Reissued by Four Courts Press, Dublin, 1992).
	Curran, Olive C.	*History of the Diocese of Meath 1860–1993* (3 vols, Meath, 1995).

Appendix 2

	Healy, John	*History of the Diocese of Meath* (2 vols, Dublin, 1908).
OSSORY	Carrigan, William	*The history and antiquities of the Diocese of Ossory* (4 vols, Dublin, 1905. Reissued by Roberts Books, Kilkenny, 1981).
RAPHOE	Maguire, Edward	*A history of the Diocese of Raphoe* (2 vols, Dublin, 1920).
TUAM	Burke, Oliver J.	*The history of the Catholic archbishops of Tuam* (Dublin, 1882).
	D'Alton, Edward A.	*History of the Archbishops of Tuam* (3 vols, Dublin, 1928).
WATERFORD & LISMORE	Power, Patrick	*Waterford and Lismore: a compendium history of the united dioceses* (Cork, 1937).
	Power, Patrick	*Parochial history of Waterford and Lismore during the 18th and 19th centuries* (Waterford, 1912).

Maynooth Research Guides for Irish Local History

IN THIS SERIES

1. Raymond Refaussé, *Church of Ireland Records*
2. Terry Dooley, *Sources for the History of Landed estates in Ireland*
3. Patrick J. Corish and David Sheehy, *Records of the Irish Catholic Church*
4. Jacinta Prunty, *Maps and Mapmaking in Local History*

Maynooth Studies in Irish Local History

IN THIS SERIES

1. Paul Connell, *Parson, Priest and Master: National Education in Co. Meath 1824–41*
2. Denis A. Cronin, *A Galway Gentleman in the Age of Improvement: Robert French of Monivea, 1716–79*
3. Brian Ó Dálaigh, *Ennis in the 18th Century: Portrait of an Urban Community*
4. Séamas Ó Maitiú, *The Humours of Donnybrook: Dublin's Famous Fair and its Suppression*
5. David Broderick, *An Early Toll-Road: The Dublin–Dunleer Turnpike, 1731–1855*
6. John Crawford, *St Catherine's Parish, Dublin 1840–1900: Portrait of a Church of Ireland Community*
7. William Gacquin, *Roscommon Before the Famine: The Parishes of Kiltoom and Cam, 1749–1845*
8. Francis Kelly, *Window on a Catholic Parish: St Mary's Granard, Co. Longford, 1933–68*
9. Charles V. Smith, *Dalkey: Society and Economy in a Small Medieval Irish Town*
10. Desmond J. O'Dowd, *Changing Times: Religion and Society in Nineteenth-Century Celbridge*
11. Proinnsíos Ó Duigneáin, *The Priest and the Protestant Woman*
12. Thomas King, *Carlow: the manor and town, 1674–1721*
13. Joseph Byrne, *War and Peace: The Survival of the Talbots of Malahide 1641–1671*
14. Bob Cullen, *Thomas L. Synnott: The Career of a Dublin Catholic 1830–70*
15. Helen Sheil, *Falling into Wretchedness: Ferbane in the late 1830s*

Maynooth Studies in Irish Local History (cont.)

16 Jim Gilligan, *Graziers and Grasslands: Portrait of a Rural Meath Community 1854–1914*

17 Miriam Lambe, *A Tipperary Estate: Castle Otway, Templederry 1750–1853*

18 Liam Clare, *Victorian Bray: A Town Adapts to Changing Times*

19 Ned McHugh, *Drogheda before the Famine: Urban Poverty in the Shadow of Privilege 1826–45*

20 Toby Barnard, *The Abduction of a Limerick Heiress: Social and political relations in mid eighteenth-century Ireland*

21 Seamus O'Brien, *Famine and Community in Mullingar Poor Law Union, 1845–1849: Mud Huts and Fat Bullocks*

22 Séamus Fitzgerald, *Mackerel and the Making of Baltimore, Co. Cork, 1879–1913*

23 Íde Ní Liatháin, *The Life and Career of P.A. McHugh, 1859–1909: A Footsoldier of the Party*

24 Miriam Moffitt, *The Church of Ireland Community of Killala and Achonry 1870–1940*

25 Ann Murtagh, *Portrait of a Westmeath Tenant Community, 1879–85: The Barbavilla Murder*

26 Jim Lenehan, *Politics and Society in Athlone, 1830–1885: A Rotten Borough*

27 Anne Coleman, *Riotous Roscommon: Social Unrest in the 1840s*

28 Maighréad Ní Mhurchadha, *The Customs and Excise service in Fingal, 1684–1765: Sober, Active and Bred to the Sea*

29 Chris Lawlor, *Canon Frederick Donovan's Dunlavin 1884–1896: A west Wicklow village in the late nineteenth century*

30 Eithne Massey, *Prior Roger Outlaw of Kilmainham*

31 Terence A.M. Dooley, *The Plight of the Monaghan Protestants, 1912–26*

32 Patricia Friel, *Frederick Trench, 1746–1836 and Heywood, Queen's County the creation of a romantic landscape*

33 Tom Hunt, *Portlaw, county Waterford 1825–76, Portrait of an industrial village and its cotton industry*

34 Brian Gurrin, *A century of struggle in Delgany and Kilcole: An exploration of the social implications of population change in north-east Wicklow, 1666–1779*